CONFESSIONS
IN THE
COURTROOM

CONFESSIONS IN THE COURTROOM

■

Lawrence S. Wrightsman
Saul M. Kassin

SAGE Publications
International Educational and Professional Publisher
Newbury Park   London   New Delhi

For information address:

SAGE Publications, Inc.
2455 Teller Road
Newbury Park, California 91320
SAGE Publications Ltd.
6 Bonhill Street
London EC2A 4PU
United Kingdom
SAGE Publications India Pvt. Ltd.
M-32 Market
Greater Kailash I
New Delhi 110 048 India

Printed in the United States of America

Library of Congress Cataloging-in-Publication Data

Wrightsman, Lawrence S.
    Confessions in the courtroom / Lawrence S. Wrightsman, Saul M.
Kassin.
       p. cm.
    Includes bibliographical references and indexes.
    ISBN 0-8039-4554-X (cl). — ISBN 0-8039-4555-8 (pb)
    1. Confession (Law)—United States. 2. Evidence, Criminal—United
States. I. Kassin, Saul M. II. Title.
    345.73'06—dc20
    [347.3056]   93-14935

93 94 95 96 97 10 9 8 7 6 5 4 3 2 1

Sage Production Editor: Astrid Virding

Contents

Preface

Problems raised by confession evidence are just as basic to the administration of criminal justice and just as important as problems with eyewitness testimony. Yet for reasons that are unclear to us, in contrast to the massive numbers of eyewitness studies, the topic of confession evidence has been almost completely ignored by psychologists and other social scientists. This book seeks to rectify that discrepancy. Our approach builds upon the methods, theories, and concepts of psychology; whether the focus is on the police methods of interrogation, their effects on suspects, or the jury's reaction to the evidence, the approach of social psychology offers a fruitful perspective.

This is an appropriate time to examine the role that confessions play in the administration of criminal justice in the United States. The U.S. Supreme Court's decision in the case *Arizona v. Fulminante,* discussed in detail in this book, has caused a reassessment of the acceptability of confessions generated under duress. Our goals in this book are, first, to examine how the legal system has, over the last half century, evolved its concept of the proper way to treat confessions, and then to examine psychological perspectives on why people confess and how other people, especially jurors, react to confessions. In looking at the causes of confessions, we carefully examine the interrogation procedures used by police. We evaluate the process for determining whether a confession should be admitted as evidence in a trial. We summarize our program of research on jurors' reactions to voluntary and coerced confessions. We attempt to assess the impact of the *Fulminante* decision on the future of these phenomena. Our aim is to provide the first comprehensive multidisciplinary account of the state of criminal confessions in the United States today. The more than 170 references we cite range from reports of psychological research to appellate court decisions to descriptions of trials by journalists. Our audience is social scientists, attorneys, and members of the justice system who seek a readable and objective treatment of this topic. Our hope is that this book will contribute to the recognition that confession evidence is not only a topic of concern to our society, but also a topic worthy of increased investigation.

Acknowledgments

This is the fourth book that the two of us have authored or edited for Sage Publications on aspects of the court system. We are indebted to C. Terry Hendrix, Senior Editor of Sage Publications, for encouraging us to develop our ideas and for identifying topics of interest to scholars and professional persons. The staff of Sage Publications continue to be a model for what a publishing company should be in regard to helpfulness to authors.

We have benefited also from the assistance of students and colleagues in the preparation of this book. At the University of Kansas, Teddy D. Warner (now on the faculty of Iowa State University) was a co-author on some of the research described in Chapter 6. Chris Bauer prepared a draft of the report on the Bernhard Goetz confession. Don Christie analyzed police manuals. Jennifer Gottschalk and Stacey Stranathan did library research and analyzed data. Laura Shaw facilitated an improvement in the description of details from the *Fulminante* case. Among the faculty, Professor Pete Rowland of the Department of Political Science clarified court decisions and Professor David Holmes brought several significant pieces of research to our attention.

At Williams College a number of students have been co-authors in the program of research described in Chapter 6; these include

Marisa E. Reddy, William F. Tulloch, Karlyn McNall, Holly Sukel, Lee Kiechel, and John Facciani.

We value the comments of K. C. Scull on Chapter 3. We are unable to list the names of all of the journalists, attorneys, and judges with whom we have discussed confessions evidence but we have learned from the opportunity to interrogate them. Of course, any errors or misinterpretations in this book are our responsibility and not that of our colleagues, students, or consultants.

Finally, a special set of thanks is offered to Katia Silva, who typed several drafts of this manuscript with unfailing enthusiasm, impressive accuracy, and unbelievable promptness.

—Lawrence S. Wrightsman
—Saul M. Kassin

O N E

Confessions in Court

Nothing has more impact on a jury in a criminal trial than evidence that the defendant confessed to the crime. In fact, J. H. Wigmore (1970), in his classic law school textbook titled *Evidence,* cited several authoritative legal scholars who confirmed his contention that a confession ranks as absolutely the most influential type of evidence.

We propose two bases for Wigmore's conclusion. First, even though estimates vary somewhat, it is clear that confession evidence is introduced with relentless regularity in the courts. A survey of deputy district attorneys in Los Angeles County, for example, revealed that confessions were a part of the testimony in 47% of the 4,000 cases surveyed (Younger, 1966). Similarly, the district attorney of New York City stated that he planned to offer confession evidence in 68% of the homicide cases that were pending there (Kaufman, 1966). Similar percentages occur in Great Britain; Baldwin and McConville (1980) found a confession rate of about 50% in London and Birmingham. Mitchell (1983) reviewed the cases of 394 defendants who came before the Worcester Crown Court in 1978; 70% had confessed to the police. Kalven and Zeisel's (1966) extensive survey of trial judges found that disputed confessions—that is, those that were later denied by the defendant or whose admissibility was challenged by the defense—arose in approximately 20% of the 3,576 criminal trials that they sampled nationwide. When we consider that

1

from 80% to 95% of criminal cases never go to trial because the defendant pleads guilty and/or plea-bargains—thus "confessing" to the commission of a crime—these figures are even more astounding. In addition to the prevalence of confession evidence, a second reason for its importance is the massive impact that it can single-handedly exert on a criminal defendant's fate. McCormick's (1972) textbook on evidence even put it this way: "The introduction of a confession makes the other aspects of a trial in court seem superfluous" (p. 316). The compelling nature of confession evidence has also been demonstrated empirically. In a mock-jury experiment, Miller and Boster (1977) had their subjects read a description of a murder trial that included (a) only circumstantial evidence, (b) eyewitness testimony from either an acquaintance or a stranger, or (c) testimony alleging that the defendant had confessed to the police. As it turned out, those subjects who received the confession evidence were more likely to view the defendant as guilty than were those in other conditions, including those provided with the eyewitness identification.

But all is not so straightforward and simple. Two problems surface, or perhaps better put, a problem and a mystery. First, confession evidence is not always valid. That is, a suspect may have confessed not because he or she actually committed the crime, but for other reasons. Or the evidence may come not from the defendant, but from a witness who claims that the defendant confessed. (At this point we need to add an important reminder: When evidence of a confession is presented in court, it is almost always a part of the testimony of the police officer who elicited the confession, not the testimony of the defendant who allegedly confessed. When exceptions to this rule occur, as in the Chico Mendes murder trial to be described later in this chapter, they usually are accounted for by motivations other than complete honesty.)

The problems with confession evidence are so common that there are numerous examples of erroneous convictions based almost exclusively on uncorroborated confession evidence. In *Convicting the Innocent,* for example, Borchard (1932) reviewed 65 criminal cases involving defendants, many of whom were incarcerated or even executed on the basis of confessions that were subsequently proved to be false. More recently, Bedau and Radelet (1987) identified 350 miscarriages of justice in which innocent persons were convicted of capital crimes in the United States. In 49 of these cases, the conviction was based on a false confession.

Second—the mystery—social scientists have given scant attention to the role of confessions evidence in determining prosecution and guilt. If, as indicated in the Miller and Boster study cited earlier, mock jurors are more influenced by testimony about a confession than by an eyewitness's identification, we are baffled by the inconsistency between the recent mass of research and writing by psychologists on eyewitness accuracy and the virtual absence of empirical study of jurors' reactions to confession evidence. For example, an examination of the *Psychological Abstracts* and the *Sociological Abstracts* indicates that neither of the 1990 volumes had any entries under "confessions." Furthermore, a check of the eight most recent textbooks on the topic of psychology and the law finds that six of these do not include the term in their subject indexes, and the recently published and comprehensive *Handbook of Psychology and Law* (Kagehiro & Laufer, 1992) includes only three brief mentions of the term.

DEFINITION OF A CONFESSION

A purpose of this book is to redress the imbalance, and to try to draw attention to the nature of confessions and their role in criminal justice. In doing so, this chapter will illustrate the complexity of the problem by describing several examples of questionable confessions and then elucidating the confession process by examining one case in detail. But first, we need to clarify what constitutes a confession. One way that the term has been defined is "an acknowledgment, in expressed words, by the accused in a criminal case, of the truth of the guilty fact charged or of some essential part of it" (Wigmore, 1970, p. 308). As we will see in the forthcoming example, "some essential part of it" is a portion of the definition not to be tossed off lightly. What a suspect confesses to may differ substantially from what he or she, as defendant, is charged with at trial.

Some commentators have viewed the above traditional definition as narrow in scope because it excludes guilty conduct (e.g., fleeing from arrest), exculpatory statements (e.g., a self-defense explanation or apology), and other admissions (i.e., those that do not bear directly on the issue of guilt or fall short of an acknowledgment of all essential elements of the crime). These distinctions, particularly that between confessions and other types of verbal admissions, had, in the past, enabled the courts to circumvent having to apply stringent rules governing the introduction of confession evidence when dealing with other types of self-incriminating statements (McCormick, 1972). However, because these distinctions are often subtle and difficult to make in individual cases (Slough, 1959) and because the U.S. Supreme Court has (until the 1991 case of *Arizona v. Fulminante*) indicated that coerced confessions are subject to the same constitutional safeguards as full confessions (e.g., *Ashcraft v. Tennessee*, 1944), today's accepted operational definition is, for all practical purposes, one that encompasses a relatively wide range of self-incriminating behaviors under the label "confession."

THE COMPLEXITY OF CONFESSIONS

To the layperson whose exposure to a suspect's confession may be brief—coming from a newspaper article or quick mention on the television news—the presence of a confession may be straightforward and require no further scrutiny. Nothing could be further from the truth. Is an alleged confession authentic? Was the defendant of sound mind or could he have confessed to crimes he did not commit? Was his statement coerced or induced by trickery during an interrogation? Was the suspect's constitutional privilege against self-incrimination violated? Can the testimony of possibly overzealous police officers be trusted?

Consider, for example, the case of Randall Adams, which was described in the film, *The Thin Blue Line*. After extensively questioning Adams (who was falsely suspected of killing a police officer), the detective typed up a statement supposedly made by Adams—but he added a confession. In court, he then produced a signed copy of the statement that Adams had refused to sign. Adams was convicted of murder and sentenced to death (Adams, Hoffer, & Hoffer, 1991).

As implied earlier, many motives exist for a sudden "confession." During routine questioning in the trial of the men accused of killing the Brazilian rain forest defender, Chico Mendes, one of the defendants, 23-year-old Darci Alves Pereira, startled the courtroom spectators by admitting that he alone had gunned down the rubber tapper on December 22, 1988. His defense attorney told the press that "he was completely surprised" by the confession. But the chief prosecuting attorney discounted the admission, concluding that it was a planned maneuver to spare Pereira's father, the other defendant, from a murder conviction. If that was the reason, it didn't work, as both the son and his father, aged 54, were found guilty of the murder and were sentenced to 19 years in prison.

But other reasons abound for confessing, especially during an interrogation by the police. Back in 1955, a woman named Nancy Parker was murdered. Her husband, David Parker, confessed but soon withdrew his confession, claiming he had been forced into it. Regardless, Parker was convicted and sentenced to spend the rest of his life in the Nebraska State Penitentiary. After serving 13 years in prison, he was released, when an appeals court ruled that his confession was, in fact, "coerced and involuntary." Meanwhile, another man, Wesley Peery, confessed to the killing of Nancy Parker. Peery, who had been questioned shortly after the murder, waited until 1977 to confess to his lawyer. Even after that delay, his admission was not revealed until after his death in 1988 (Associated Press, 1989).

Did, in fact, the husband of the victim confess only after intense pressure to do so? We all can think of famous examples—Galileo, for one—whose coerced confessions were not sincere. Or, on the other hand, was it the latter-day confession of Wesley Peery that should be suspect? It was, after all, given while Peery was on death row, expressed in the hopes that a profitable book would be written about his exploits. All we can say for sure is that two confessions exist to the same crime, and only one can be correct.

Consider another example. Johnny Wilson is a mentally retarded person, with the mental capacity of a third-grader. In 1986, at the age of 20, he confessed to the murder of Pauline Martz, a businesswoman in Aurora, MO. He later claimed that he confessed only after a late-night, 6-hour interrogation, so that he could go home and get away from the police officer who had been abusive during the questioning. "I didn't like what they were doing to me, and the only way to get out of there was to confess," he said; "As soon as they locked me up, I thought, 'I'm in deep trouble now' " (quoted in Spivak, 1988, p. 314). After entering a so-called Alford plea (in which he did not admit guilt but acknowledged that the prosecution had enough evidence for a conviction), Wilson was sentenced to life in prison. Like the previous example, an inmate in another prison has confessed to the murder for which Wilson is serving a life sentence. This case highlights the question whether high-powered police interrogation techniques serve the course of justice when they are applied to mentally retarded or emotionally disturbed suspects. At the very least, the use of these techniques increases the risk of false confessions and erroneous convictions.

What is missing in most accounts of a "confession" are the specifics—important specifics such as just what was admitted, how it was elicited, and why it was made. The following detailed example of an actual case fills in some gaps but also illustrates how we usually don't know the answer to some important questions about the nature of a confession.

THE CONFESSION OF BRIAN KEITH BELL

As Frank Seurer, Sr., left the Village Inn in Lawrence, KS, on August 2, 1983, after drinking his early-morning coffee, he had good feelings about the future. And why not; fall football practice at the University of Kansas was about to begin, and Mr. Seurer's son was the first-string quarterback on the Jayhawks football team. In fact, Frank Jr., a senior who had started as the KU quarterback for 3 years and led them to one bowl game, had already been picked as a second-team All-American on one national preseason team. Frank Seurer, Sr., had been so excited about his son's future that in January he had moved his family from Huntington Beach, CA, to Lawrence.

He and his wife had bought a local barbecue restaurant close to the campus and had re-named it Pop's Bar-B-Q.

So there was ample reason for Frank Seurer to be joyous as he finished his morning coffee on August 2. But within 2 hours he would be dead. He was found lying on the floor of his restaurant kitchen about 9:30 that morning; the autopsy later revealed that he had been stabbed 23 times, including 6 times in the chest, 3 times around his upper arm, and 14 times in the back. Apparently two different instruments had been used, although neither was ever discovered. A total of $446 in bills and coins had been stolen from the cash register.

On August 17, 2½ weeks after the crime, a young man named Keith Bell, age 23, was brought in for questioning. The police had been well aware of Keith Bell, who used to be an employee of the restaurant. He was a nephew of the previous owner of the restaurant, Bobby Bell, a former player with the Kansas City Chiefs and member of the National Football League Hall of Fame. In fact, Keith Bell had worked there while his uncle owned it, and had continued to after the sale. (Mrs. Sue Seurer later testified, "Keith taught us how to run the barbecue business.") But Keith was no longer employed there on the day of the murder. However, he had attended Mr. Seurer's funeral and afterward drove around with Beth Seurer, the victim's daughter, trying to calm her. His solicitousness led him to offer to help out at the restaurant again after the owner's death.

Keith Bell had become a suspect because his fingerprints were on two envelopes found at the scene of the crime. The envelopes were addressed to his uncle, care of the restaurant, and the police determined that they had been mailed after Keith's last reported visit to the restaurant. Thus, the Lawrence police suspected Bell of the murder, as the envelopes were discovered lying on the kitchen floor next to Mr. Seurer's body. The police speculated that on August 2, Keith Bell had gone to the restaurant to ask Mr. Seurer for his job back, that Seurer had given him the two letters addressed to Keith's uncle, and that, for some reason, an argument had developed.

After 6½ hours of continuous questioning on August 17, Keith Bell signed a statement confessing that he had stabbed Frank Seurer *two or three times.* He was then charged with second-degree murder and aggravated robbery.

Before evidence about a confession can be introduced at trial, a hearing is held to determine if the confession was elicited involuntarily. If so, the jurors cannot be told about the confession. A judge— usually the one who will preside at the jury trial—listens to the police officers who did the questioning describe the interrogation procedure; then the judge decides whether or not the confession can be admitted into evidence. At the hearing regarding Keith Bell's confession, a police detective testified under oath about the number of occasions on which Bell was questioned, the length of each interrogation, the type of room in which they were held, the number of people present, and the number of breaks and what was done during each. This preliminary hearing lasted about an hour; Bell's attorney was allowed to cross-examine the police officer. No audio or videotape of the questioning was presented.

The police detective told the judge that he first interviewed Brian Keith Bell about 3 p.m. the day of the murder.

"Did you advise him of his Miranda rights?"

"On that occasion, no. It was not a custodial interview; he was not a suspect, in my mind. He was a past employee who had shown up at the scene of the crime." Cross-examination elicited the detective's acknowledgment that at that point he did not ask Bell if he had committed the crime.

The police officer went on: "He was not under arrest; he was free to leave. He didn't ask to leave, didn't ask to stop, didn't ask for an attorney. His answers were generally responsive." The detective did take his fingerprints. This initial questioning lasted almost 3 hours, perhaps a testimonial to the police department's thoroughness if—as they claimed—Bell was not at that time a suspect.

During the next several weeks the police apparently questioned Bell briefly and informally several times. The police detectives began eating lunch at Pop's Bar-B-Q; Keith was often around. They also asked him to take a polygraph examination; he initially agreed to but withdrew during the examination.

The interview that generated Bell's confession took place on August 17, a little more than 2 weeks after the crime. Again the locale was the conference room of the sheriff's office. Bell was questioned again because of the two letters, addressed to Bobby Bell in care of the restaurant, that were found next to Frank Seurer's body; latent fingerprints on the envelopes were Keith Bell's. So, by the time of this final questioning, the police had begun to concentrate their investigation on Bell.

This time the police did read Bell his Miranda rights. He signed the form without reluctance. The questioning began about 3:20 p.m. At about 7 p.m. Bell agreed to give a statement; after he did so, it was typed up and he signed it. Bell was put in a jail cell about 9 p.m. During this almost-6-hour period there were four breaks, for such purposes as getting a drink, going to the bathroom, and taking an aspirin. The detective testified that Bell was offered something to eat, but declined.

Shortly after the questioning began, the two detectives told Bell they disbelieved what he had been telling them. He was told about his fingerprints being on the envelopes. Twice, early in the interview, he refused to say that he had struck Mr. Seurer. But he expressed concern that he was going to be charged with a crime or sent to jail. He worried about what the newspapers would say, and felt bad about the embarrassment to his uncle.

As the interaction wound on, the detectives once again asked him if he was guilty and "he said he was." This admission was not videotaped; nor was a court reporter present.

According to the detective, Bell acknowledged that he had stopped by at the Seurer's restaurant the morning of the murder. At one point during the questioning—after making this admission—he asked the police detectives what would happen if he confirmed that he had stabbed Mr. Seurer. The detectives told him that was up to the district attorney. Finally, Keith Bell told the detectives his version of what happened: he had stopped by during his morning jogging to ask for his job back. He told Mr. Seurer that he was short of money and that his rent was overdue. His former boss turned him down, and then made what Keith Bell felt was a racial slur, something to the effect of "You colored boys never can manage your money." An argument ensued, and according to Bell, Seurer bumped him and reached for a knife. (They were in the kitchen of the restaurant.) Bell grabbed a knife, too, and stabbed the older man twice. And he signed a statement to that effect.

Bell did not testify at the hearing that was held to determine the admissibility of his confession. After listening to the testimony of the detectives and the cross-examination by Bell's attorney, the judge ruled that the confession was voluntary and hence was admissible into evidence. At this point the news media announced that Bell "had confessed."

Note that Bell never confessed to "murder." He signed a statement that he struck Mr. Seurer only "two or three times" and only as result of an argument emanating from a racial slur. But the jury never heard his story, as we will see later. The newspaper and television reports that he "confessed to murder" were misleading. Stories in the media portraying Mr. Seurer having been stabbed more than 20 times, in the back and in the chest, with two different knives, were juxtaposed with accounts of Bell's confession, leading the public to assume that he confessed to all of these specific facts. In actuality, when the detectives told Bell about the number of knife wounds, he claimed to be surprised; "There's some sick son of a bitch out there," he told them.

Despite the fact that the killing and the confession spanned the dog days of August and that they occurred while much of this college town was "closed down" between summer school and the beginning of the fall semester, Mr. Seurer's murder was the topic of much local conversation and speculation. And the wire services even spread the news of the murder across the country.

Guarded conversations must have increased after local newspapers published accounts of the preliminary hearing held on the first day of September. Susan Seurer, widow of the victim, testified that she had fired Keith Bell on June 30 because he had refused to wash the dishes as part of his job duties. Furthermore, she testified that Keith Bell recently told her that he had carried on an affair with Beth Seurer, who was then 18 years old. Bell had told Mrs. Seurer that her daughter had had an abortion. But Mrs. Seurer never informed her husband. The Seurer's are white; Bell is black—a point of relevance later in the trial.

Thus, when 28 Lawrence citizens were called for jury duty on Monday, November 7, 1983, probably most or all of them knew the purpose of this trial, because local and Kansas City papers had—over the last week—printed several stories about the upcoming trial. For example, any prospective jurors who were careful readers of the newspapers (or TV news watchers) would have already learned that Bell's attorney had tried to prevent the introduction of the confession into evidence, but the judge had ruled it admissible. They probably knew that, despite the confession, Bell was pleading not guilty to the charges. A news story 3 days before the trial headlined: "Bell's attorney says insanity will not be used as a defense."

So, many jurors knew what to expect, and probably faced their task with dread, excitement, or a combination of both. After all, they had to make a decision in a case of apparent murder, involving several local celebrities, in which illicit interracial sex was possibly a contributing factor.

But, officially, the facts of the trial were only gradually revealed to the prospective jurors. It was 30 minutes after they had been ushered into the courtroom that they formally learned the nature of the case. The district attorney told them that "the defendant is charged with stabbing his former employer in the back and in the heart and he died. He is also charged with taking money." Prior to that, they had received a brief orientation from the administrative judge, but he had not told them the nature of the first case that they were to adjudicate. (Jurors in this county serve for a month at a time.) The administrative judge did instruct them not to read newspapers or watch TV newscasts during the trial, and he explained the distinction between peremptory challenges and challenges for cause that would emerge during the jury-selection process.

The administrative judge discouraged jurors from taking notes during the trial presentation. "Sometimes persons taking notes will miss evidence coming from the witness stand. Another reason is that when you are in the jury room, there may be too much reliance on notes," he said. "However, if you feel you can do better by taking notes, you can request that of Judge Elwell (the presiding judge)." No jurors chose to do so.

A JURY TRIAL FROM THE JURORS' PERSPECTIVE

It is instructive to spend some time describing this trial from the viewpoint of the jurors. All of them probably knew that they had been called as a part of a "random process," although fewer were aware that voter registration lists were the sources of names in this county. As they looked around at each other, they could note that among the 28 of them, there were somewhat more women than men, there were people of differing ages, but there were no blacks, Orientals, or Native Americans. They may have wondered if it made any difference that some were seated in the jury box and others were in the audience. (It didn't.) As the trial proceedings got closer, various people came in and took seats. "There's the defendant, escorted by the sheriff," some may have noted. He was a tall, nice-looking young man, dressed in a three-piece suit. They may have concluded that it was his parents, plus his sister, seated in the audience but as close to the defense table as they could be. And they might have spotted the victim's family—his widow, his daughter, and sons (including the football star)—across the middle aisle in the small courtroom.

As the trial began, the prospective jurors heard the clerk call out their names; a sort of roll was taken. The district attorney was helpful. He introduced all the officers of the court, and, as we noted, he was the first person to tell them officially what they had already assumed.

The district attorney warned them that it would "take a while to select the jury;" actually, the voir dire was completed by noon of the first day. He read a list of 25 possible witnesses and asked the group, en masse, if anyone knew any of them. As individuals put their hands up, they were questioned about the extent of their knowledge and their ability to remain impartial. It developed that one prospective juror ate frequently at Pops Bar-B-Q; he was quickly excused for cause. Several others knew central persons in the case or in the Seurer family, but up to the midpoint of the jury selection, only 2 of the 28 had been excused for cause—both after they had stated that they were sure they couldn't be fair because of their involvement with the Seurers.

But about halfway through the jury selection, something unusual happened. In contrast to the usual docility of jurors, one of the prospective jurors seated in the audience said, "Someone is not being honest." The district attorney had just described the standard of reasonable doubt and had asked the group if they could subscribe to it without difficulty. The prospective juror reported that another member of the panel, seated behind her, had said, "This is a joke." The judge immediately called a recess and asked to see several of the prospective jurors in his chambers. As the questioning resumed about 15 minutes later, the rest of the prospective jurors could not help but notice that another member of their group was gone. (The panel member who reported the comment was still there, but she was not chosen for the actual jury.)

The prospective jurors heard the district attorney intersperse mini-lectures among his questions to them. For example, he told them about the difference between physical evidence and circumstantial evidence, using the example of a "missing" canary and a contented cat that now sits in the canary's cage among some bird feathers. "There's nothing wrong with circumstantial evidence," he said. "The fact that there isn't dramatic scientific evidence doesn't mean you can't find guilt beyond a reasonable doubt. Does everybody understand that?" he asked.

He also tried to warn them that some photographs would be introduced that "frankly aren't very pretty." The panel was asked if anyone might become too upset. No one said so. But perhaps some of them took it as a message about the serious business they were going to be dealing with.

The district attorney noted that there had been some publicity about the crime on the radio and TV and in the newspapers. All but one prospective juror acknowledged that they had read or heard something about the case. (Interestingly, that one person was among those chosen for the jury.) "Can each of you put aside what you have read, heard, or seen, and base your decision solely on the evidence?" No one volunteered that he or she couldn't.

"Does the fact that the defendant is a black American, a black male, make it difficult for anyone to be fair?" No one said so. Matter closed.

Throughout his 2 hours of questioning, the district attorney treated the prospective jurors with courtesy and concern. He knew their names (from a seating chart), used their names, and made sure to pronounce them correctly. At one point he apologized for taking so long, revealing a sheepish smile. At 11:00 a.m., he announced his "last question"; "When the judge tells you the law, it is your duty to apply the law even if you have personal disagreements with the law. Do you understand that?" With the possible exception of a couple of law students who were on the panel, no one knew that a jury nullification instruction was applicable in some states, whereby jurors were told that they could disregard the law. No one objected, including the defendant's attorney.

Now it was time for the defense to take center stage in the jury selection process. The defense attorney was briefer in his questioning, and in many other ways the jurors must have felt that he was a sharp contrast to the district attorney. An overweight middle-aged white man with a rumpled look and untidy curly hair, he told these Kansas jurors that he was from Kansas City, *Missouri,* and asked if any of them were prejudiced against him because of his home state. Whether this was a serious concern on his part or an attempt at icebreaking humor, the jurors failed to show any discernible response.

The defense attorney persisted: "The TV has some lawyer shows. Any one expect me to break down a witness or be like Perry Mason?" No response from the panel, although many of them were probably becoming offended.

The defense attorney consistently mispronounced the name of the victim, calling him Frank "SOUR", Sr. (it is pronounced "SIGH-er"), to the audible annoyance of the victim's family. Was this intentional, some jurors may have wondered.

But that was not all. He asked the jurors if they were Kansas University football fans. Lawrence being the home of KU, anyone would have assumed that most of them were. "I'm not much of a KU fan," the defense attorney gratuitously added.

The defense attorney told the two law students on the panel that "its not too late to change occupations," and he dealt with the "problem" of how to address women, by arrogantly announcing to the panel that when referring to them, "I call all ladies 'Missus'; that way I don't have a problem."

But he did have a problem with some jurors' names; in fact, his garbled pronunciation of one juror's name became the standing joke of the voir dire portion of the trial.

In less than an hour's time the defense attorney had offended practically everyone on the jury panel. But at 11:55 a.m., his questioning mercifully ended. The judge gave the two attorneys only 4 minutes to decide which panel members would receive their peremptory challenges. (Each side had six.) After a few minutes devoted to collating the lists, the clerk announced the names of the prospective jurors who "could leave." Those panel members had no way of knowing why they weren't chosen for the jury. Twelve remained— four men and eight women; they did not include the law students or the woman who had blown the whistle on her colleague.

We can imagine that during the period of waiting, jurors had individually reviewed their reactions to the trial so far. Were they unconsciously influenced by the contrasting styles of the two attorneys? Could the pretrial publicity have established an expectation of guilt? How many knew already that the defendant had "confessed"? Neither side asked the prospective jurors during voir dire if they had heard or read anything about a confession.

The trial presentation itself took 3 days (Monday afternoon through Thursday morning). After the district attorney made an 8-minute opening statement, the defense attorney announced that he would waive his right to make an opening statement until later, thus denying the jury the opportunity to have an alternative scenario by which they might organize the facts of the case.

The prosecution introduced a variety of witnesses, including the police detectives who investigated the crime scene and later obtained a confession from the defendant, the coroner who described the nature of the 23 stab wounds, and a former woman friend (white) of the defendant who testified that she had visited Keith Bell on August 18 while he was in jail and that he had told her that he had stabbed the victim "once or twice."

The prosecution took 2½ days to present its evidence. In one sense, it looked convincing; there was Keith Bell's signed statement confessing that he had stabbed Mr. Seurer "two or three times." His fingerprints were on two envelopes found near the body. And police found a jar of coins under the sink in his apartment.

But there were a number of weak aspects to the prosecution's case, as well as some unanswered questions. For example, the expert from the Kansas Bureau of Investigation had never testified before about fingerprints, and her responses about her procedures didn't inspire confidence. And it sounded surprising, given all the people who must have handled the two pieces of mail, that Keith Bell's fingerprints were the only ones that could be discerned on the envelopes.

And why did Keith do it, if he did? The detective who took his confession reported—as he did in the preliminary hearing—that Keith said he had stopped by the restaurant early that morning while he was jogging. He had asked Mr. Seurer for his job back, telling him that he was behind in his rent payments. Mr. Seurer snickered; apparently he told Bell, "I can't understand why you colored guys can't manage your money." Bell remembered that Mr. Seurer had pushed him, or maybe bumped him. The detective testified:

> Something snapped. Keith Bell hit him a couple of times. He said he stabbed him in the back once or twice, and then Frank Seurer Sr. turned and Keith Bell said he hit him again in the chest. Seurer said: "What are you doing?" As he slumped to the floor, he said, "You're killing me."

Bell told the detective he then picked up two money bags, took the money from the cash register, and left. He insisted to the police that he had only stabbed Mr. Seurer two or three times, and apparently believed that someone else must have come in to finish the job, if there really were as many as 23 separate stab wounds.

Although all of this is quite plausible, it came from the testimony of the detective, *not directly from Bell*. The jurors must have looked forward to hearing the defendant's side of the story. Was he provoked into an attack? Or did he now claim that he hadn't done it at all? And then there was the mystery of his behavior later that day, and in the next few days.

For one of the prosecution witnesses, Clarence Ackland, had testified that he had been awakened by a phone call from Keith Bell around 8:30-9:00 a.m. the day of the murder. (In fact, this was just about the time when the crime occurred.) Ackland reported that Keith's car wouldn't start. An engineering student at KU, Ackland helped Bell get the car going, but water was gushing out of the water pump. They drove in their separate cars to an Amoco station about two blocks from Pop's Bar-B-Q, where Bell left the car for repairs about 9 a.m. Later, a mechanic at that service station testified that Bell came back around noon to pick up the car. But he was back with the car about 1:30 p.m. with another problem. Is this the behavior of a man who has just killed his former employer? And the jurors already knew, from the testimony of another prosecution witness, that Keith Bell had consoled the daughter of the victim the night after the murder, and even attended the funeral.

So, as the prosecution rested its case about 3:30 p.m. on the third day of the trial, the jurors eagerly awaited the opening statement by the defense and the testimony of the defendant. But they waited in vain.

After requesting a directed verdict of not guilty—which the judge immediately denied—the defense attorney waived his opportunity to present a defense. The jurors were left with their mouths collectively hanging open. Suddenly the trial was almost over. Only the judge's instructions and the closing arguments remained, before the jury would have to decide.

This synopsis of Keith Bell's trial summarizes some of the problems encountered in presenting information about so-called confessions to a jury. Even though jurors are supposed to disregard any information they have acquired prior to the trial, it is impossible to eliminate pretrial bias, and publicity sets up certain expectations that are hard to put aside. Almost all the publicity released prior to the trial favors the prosecution's side. And we have already mentioned the indications that information about a confession is the most damaging of all the pretrial publicity.

The jury took 4 hours to deliberate, and then brought forth a unanimous verdict that Bell was guilty of second-degree homicide and aggravated robbery. The result was not surprising.

Was justice served? Did the jurors bring down the correct verdict? The evidence was overwhelming that Keith Bell's actions caused the death of Frank Seurer, Sr. Whether or not his attorney's offensive behavior had colored their decision, Bell was clearly the perpetrator of some criminal acts. But the failure of any defense opening statement or of the defendant to testify prevented the jury's having an opportunity to weigh alternatives, especially a conviction for the commission of lesser crimes. Had these been present, there might have emerged jury acceptance of a second scenario—one that might have proposed that (a) Mr. Seurer made a racial slur, (b) Bell perceived Mr. Seurer to reach for a knife, (c) Bell grabbed a knife and struck in self-defense. A verdict finding Bell guilty only of manslaughter could have legitimately resulted if the jury had heard Bell testify to his version of the facts. Furthermore, the failure to testify meant that, by default, the jury had only one version of the police interrogation of Keith Bell.

RECURRING THEMES

This case illustrates several phenomena that will recur throughout this book:

1. If police interrogation results in a confession, a discrepancy may still exist between the acts acknowledged by the defendant in the written statement and the charges brought against the defendant at trial.

2. A "confession" is rarely spontaneous. It is usually negotiated, and we often don't know what the police said, did, or implied in order to induce it.

3. The confession is almost always presented to the decision maker—whether the judge ruling on its voluntariness or the jury on the guilt of the defendant—by the prosecution, not by the defendant.

4. Once a confession has been introduced into testimony, attempts to rebut it are largely futile. (The trial of Bernhard Goetz, described later in this book, is a notorious exception to this rule.)

5. Unless a videotape of the *entire interrogation* is introduced into the evidence, decision makers may form incorrect inferences about the motives for confessing. Police sometimes test the limits in leading suspects to expect clemency or leniency if they confess, without actually promising such.

OVERVIEW OF THE BOOK

The purpose of this book is to describe and evaluate what we know about confessions given to police and their impact at the subsequent trial. To give historical perspective, Chapter 2 traces the legal system's changing view of the relationship of confessions to guilt over the past 500 years.

Chapter 3 reviews the current legal status of confessions in the United States, by reviewing case law and recent Supreme Court decisions. The period from 1960 through 1990 was an extremely fertile one, with the *Miranda* decision leading to changes and reinterpretations. The 1991 *Fulminante* appeal, in which Chief Justice Rehnquist labeled admission of a coerced confession as possibly a "harmless error," is analyzed in detail in this chapter. Police interrogation procedures are explored in Chapter 4; emphasis is placed on whether they comply with current court regulations and standards of fairness. Why do people confess? Chapter 5 examines the psychological theorizing that provides hypotheses in response to this question. We offer our system for conceptualizing and understanding confessions, building on two basic distinctions between (a) true and false confessions, and (b) coercive and noncoercive interrogations.

Chapter 6 describes the authors' program of research on jurors' reactions to confessions that differ in the degree of their voluntariness, and Chapter 7 reviews the role of the social scientists as expert witnesses in trial involving confessions. The concluding chapter speculates about the future of confessions evidence in our courts as well as proposing new directions for research.

T W O

The Law

A Historical View

Confession evidence has always been a recurring source of controversy in English and American jurisprudence, as the courts have sought a balance between the need to punish perpetrators and the assumption that a suspect is innocent until proven guilty. Stephens (1973) articulated a collateral dilemma: Whether our criminal justice system, which assumes the innocence of defendants and requires the government to prove their guilt, is consistent with a practice that permits police to hold a suspect incommunicado and to introduce into evidence statements made under circumstances known only to the accuser and the accused.

According to Wigmore's (1970) historical analysis, the contemporary legal system's use of confessions has evolved through a series of discrete stages. During the 16th and 17th centuries, in England, absolutely no restrictions existed about excluding confessions. All avowals of self-guilt were accepted at face value, without discrimination. In fact, they were equivalent to the plea of guilt, precluding the need for a formal trial. One statement, in 1607, said it succinctly: "a confession is a conviction" (cited in Wigmore, 1970. p. 293).

SHIFTS IN ENGLISH JURISPRUDENCE

Wigmore observed that at least through the middle of the 17th century, the use of physical inducements to confess was the rule, and the evidence so obtained was accepted without question. He noted, "Up to the middle of the 1600's, at least, the use of torture to extract confessions was common, and . . . confessions so obtained were employed evidently without scruple" (1970, p. 294).

But about this time—actually during the reign of Charles I, 1625-1649—the right against self-incrimination emerged in English common law, "largely in response to repressive measures taken, in the name of law, against some of the king's most persistent critics" (Stephens, 1973, p. 19).

Beginning with the period after the Restoration of 1660, there was a slow and gradual improvement in the procedures used in criminal trials in England. But not until one hundred years later, in 1775, in *Rudd's case,* did a judge for the first time place any restrictions on the admissibility of an ordinary confession. And shortly after that, in 1783, the modern view on the admissibility of confessions received what Wigmore (1970) called a "full and clear expression," that is, that confessions that were obtained through promises or threats were not to receive credit as evidence.

At this point in his historical narrative Wigmore made a rather astounding statement, given the continuing controversy over the admissibility of coerced confessions: "From this time on (i.e., 1783), the history of the doctrine is merely a matter of the narrowness or broadness of the exclusionary rule" (1970, p. 297). The point is—and Wigmore himself acknowledged it—that even while the doctrine was espoused that apparently untrustworthy confessions should not be accepted as indications of guilt, in the late 1700s very few confessions were in fact excluded from evidence. The everyday procedures were not consistent with the judicial precedents.

In contrast, by the beginning of the 19th century, a time emerged during which the judiciary was generally cynical about all confessions and tended to repudiate them if given the slightest justification. Two bases for this distrust of confessions were articulated—(a) that the process of procuring proof of an alleged confession through the testimony of a victim, informer, or police officer is of questionable reliability; and (b) even when the confession is a well-proven fact, it may have little diagnostic value (as an indicator of guilt) if coerced or induced by promises, threats, or other tactics of the "third degree." This latter concern about the danger of false admissions was so extreme that Wigmore cited, as an example of a reason that a confession was excluded, that "it was made upon a promise to give a glass of gin" (1970, p. 297).

Doubtless the movement toward the recognition of human dignity and individuality that swept the European continent and North America in the late 1700s contributed to this shift. One significant improvement was permitting the accused to testify in his or her own behalf—in order to attempt to discredit the confession previously given. As Wigmore stated, this development was in response to the unfairness of a system that had virtually told the person, "You cannot be trusted to speak here or elsewhere in your own behalf, but we shall use against you whatever you may have said" (1970, p. 300).

U.S. SUPREME COURT DECISIONS
IN THE EARLY 1900s

In a thorough review of U.S. Supreme Court decisions regarding confessions, Otis H. Stephens, Jr. (1973), observed that the initial concern of the Court, in the early 1900s, was toward the "third degree" practices of the police (see Chapter 4). What resulted as the most common legal sanction against inappropriate police questioning was to challenge the admissibility of the evidence thus obtained. But the Supreme Court has also encouraged other safeguards; see Box 2.1.

Prior to the 1960s, when the Supreme Court led by Chief Justice Earl Warren instituted major reforms, the basis of the Supreme Court's skeptical view toward admitting out-of-court confessions in state prosecutions was the broad requirements of the Due Process Clause of the Fourteenth Amendment to the U.S. Constitution. Emphasis was thus placed on the "voluntariness" of a challenged statement, the alleged circumstances of coercion, and the supposed ability

BOX 2.1
Corroboration as a Requirement Against False Confessions

Stephens (1973) notes: "In addition to its development of safe-guards against coerced confessions, the Supreme Court has also endorsed the evidentiary rule requiring corroboration of any extra-judicial confession, admission, or other statement made by the defendant and later introduced as evidence of guilt. Two variations of this rule have emerged: one stressing corroboration of the truth or reliability of the confession; the other requiring independent proof 'tending' to establish the corpus delicti, that is the fact that the crime charged has been committed" (p. 13). The second rule is of less protection to the defendant, of course, but the first definition of corroboration is an important safeguard against accepting co-erced confessions. Unfortunately for defendants' rights, most American courts have tended to favor the latter application of the rule, but "nothing approaching unanimity has been reached, and confusion seems to have been produced by failure to differentiate clearly between these two formulations of the rule" (Stephens, 1973, p. 13).

of the suspect to withstand pressure from the police (Stephens, 1973). Since the 1930s, the Supreme Court has spoken with unanim-ity in its condemnation of *extreme* forms of police "third-degree" methods. The *Brown v. Mississippi* case, decided in 1936, is a prime example; it is described in Box 2.2.

Until the 1960s, however, the Court was divided in its opinion about the kind of police pressure that was less drastic than the use of physical force or overt threats. As Stephens noted,

Intra-Court disagreement has also risen over the point separat-ing legitimate interrogation from unconstitutional coercion. Some justices (frequently a majority) have maintained that this distinc-tion should be made largely on the basis of the individual suspect's supposed ability to withstand the pressure of police questioning. Other members of the Court have insisted on con-demning as "inherently coercive" sessions of interrogation that

BOX 2.2
Brown v. Mississippi: A Pivotal Case

Brown v. Mississippi (1936) became a pivotal case for several reasons. First, the Court reversed a guilty verdict because of a confession that was obtained through physical brutality, and its decision asserted that a trial is a mere pretense when the state authorities have contrived a conviction resting solely upon confessions obtained by violence. Without the forced confessions of the three defendants there was little if any evidence upon which to convict them of murder (Stephens, 1973).

The crime in the *Brown* case occurred in March 1934; a white man, a farmer, in Kemper County, MS, was found in his home, brutally murdered. A blood-stained axe and an article of clothing with gray hairs and blood on it were found near the house of one of the defendants, Henry Shields. A deputy sheriff and a mob of vigilantes took one of the other subsequent defendants, Yank Ellington, to the victim's house and hanged him from the limb of a tree. Taken down, he persisted in disclaiming any part in the murder. He was hanged a second time, and also whipped severely, but did not change his story. The mob released him but 2 days later two sheriff's deputies beat him again. At last, he agreed to sign whatever statement the sheriff wished to dictate. The other two defendants, the above-named Shields and Ed Brown, were put in jail, where they were severely whipped with a leather strap to which metal buckles were attached. Told that this torture would continue until they admitted guilt, they confessed—and even altered the details of their confessions to fit the demands of their inquisitors. Within 1 week of the confessions, the three defendants were found guilty and sentenced to death. These convictions were affirmed twice by the Mississippi Supreme Court (although on both occasions powerful and persuasive dissenting opinions were filed), before the U.S. Supreme Court overturned them.

exceed a given number of hours or (prior to *Miranda*) occur in the absence of formal warnings of the right to remain silent and the right to the presence of an attorney. (1973, p. 16)

The specification of a given number of hours—first used in *Ashcraft v. Tennessee* 1944, by Justice Hugo Black—is an interesting procedure, given the Supreme Court's usual aversion to quantifying what are acceptable procedures in the criminal justice system. In this case, E. E. Ashcraft had been questioned continuously for 36 hours in connection with his wife's murder. Interrogated by police officers "in relays," he was given only 5 minutes' respite from questioning during this entire period. Writing for the six-justice majority, Justice Black did not attempt to assess the impact of this prolonged questioning of Ashcraft. Rather, he declared that the intensity and duration of the interrogation constituted a "situation . . . so inherently coercive that its very existence is irreconcilable with the possession of mental freedom by a lone suspect against whom its full coercive force is brought to bear" (*Ashcraft v. Tennessee,* p. 154).

The *Ashcraft* appeal was the first in which the Supreme Court reviewed a state confession case and focused on the *process* of private interrogation. Although the justices did not find the process, as such, unconstitutional, they did insist that it conform to those constitutional requirements that put limits on the length and intensity of questioning (Stephens, 1973). In his majority opinion, Justice Black labeled the long interrogation as "inherently coercive," but not all justices agreed. In a minority opinion, Justice Robert Jackson stated:

> The Court bases its decision on the premise that custody and examination of a prisoner for thirty-six hours is "inherently coercive." Of course it is. And so is custody and examination for one hour. Arrest itself is inherently coercive, and so is detention. . . . But does the Constitution prohibit the use of all confessions made after arrest because questioning, while one is deprived of freedom, is "inherently coercive?" The Court does not quite say so, but it is moving far and fast in that direction. (*Ashcraft v. Tennessee,* p. 161)

Justice Jackson preferred the traditional conception with its assumption that the individual suspect possessed the ability and the will to withstand pressure.

The continuing shifts in viewpoint alluded to by Wigmore's analysis at the beginning of this chapter is reflected in the decision by the Court in the case of *Lyons v. Oklahoma* (1944), decided just a little more than a month after *Ashcraft,* but with a radically different outcome. This time, Justice Jackson's view prevailed. The majority decision upheld the use of continued questioning, as long as the individual suspect possessed "mental freedom" at the time of his confession.

The juxtaposition of the *Ashcraft* decision and the one in the *Lyons* case reflects the dilemma between prohibiting "inherent coerciveness" while not frustrating the police from obtaining credible confessions. Yet it should be noted that when the Supreme Court, in the 1930s and 1940s, did restrict the admissibility of confessions, the rationale bore little resemblance to the original English common-law rule. As Stephens notes:

> The common-law rule was designed primarily to guard against the introduction of unreliable evidence. It was based on the assumption that a criminal suspect subjected to threats or other forms of intimidation might make a false confession to save himself from further coercion. The common-law rule was thus aimed not at objectionable interrogation practices *per se,* but at the protection of the defendant against an erroneous conviction. The Supreme Court, on the other hand, has been more concerned with the basic fairness of the proceedings against the individual, irrespective of the authenticity of any statement resulting from interrogation. (1973, p. 17)

DUAL OBJECTIVES

As the previous section reflects, the Court has vacillated between dual objectives. Despite this, voluntariness has emerged as a criterion for the admissibility of confession evidence. The major task for legal scholars became to articulate the theoretical rationale for this criterion as well as a procedural strategy for its implementation. Why *are* involuntary confessions excluded? Through the various Supreme Court decisions, essentially two types of reasons were advanced. First is the above-mentioned common-law explanation that involuntary confessions, like testimony given while intoxicated or in response to leading questions, are untrustworthy and unreliable (see Wigmore, 1970; *Stein v. New York,* 1953). Accordingly, the operational test recommended for judges' rulings of admissibility would be whether the inducement had been sufficient to preclude a "free and rational choice" and produce a fair risk of false confession. The second rationale, first articulated in *Lisenba v. California* (1941), is that "the aim of the requirement of due process is not to exclude presumptively false evidence but to prevent fundamental unfairness in the use of evidence whether true or false" (p. 219). Both scholarly sentiment (McCormick, 1946; Paulsen, 1954) and subsequent case law (e.g., *Rogers v. Richmond,* 1961) have shifted toward this latter emphasis on constitutionally based procedural fairness, individual rights, and the deterrence of reprehensible police misconduct. As such, although involuntary confessions may be excluded if they are seen as untrustworthy, that criterion is not enough—they must also be excluded if illegally obtained.

THE VOLUNTARINESS CRITERION

Voluntariness is a difficult concept to operationalize, because it requires inferences about the suspect's subjective state of mind and embraces the dual concerns for trustworthiness and due process. For example, voluntariness cannot be equated with the probable truth of a confession because the use of this definition could result in the failure to enforce the Due Process Clause of the Fourteenth Amendment (i.e., in instances in which confessions are coerced but subsequently corroborated by additional testimony). Many courts had adopted a rule-of-thumb approach by which confessions were excluded if induced by a "threat" or "promise." This definition is inadequate because it fails to account for other tactics of coercive interrogation that do not involve promises or threats (e.g., prolonged detention). Still other courts defined voluntariness as a subjective state of mind and attempted to assess whether the confession was free and rational or "the offspring of a reasoned choice" (*United States v. Mitchell,* 1944). As Justice Frankfurter noted, "because the

concept of voluntariness is one which concerns a mental state, there is
the imaginative recreation, largely inferential, of internal, 'psychological' fact" (*Culombe v. Connecticut,* 1961, p. 603).
Graham's (1970) review noted that in the 3 decades between
Brown v. Mississippi in 1936 and *Miranda v. Arizona* in 1966, the
Supreme Court generated 36 opinions on the voluntariness of state
court confessions. He concludes: "They covered a wide variety of
circumstances; some confessions were upheld and others were thrown
out. The result was that state courts could examine the case-by-case
authorities of the Supreme Court and could find authority for affirming
or rejecting almost any type of confession" (Graham, 1970, p. 35).
The Supreme Court, in fact, has evaded precise definition and
stated in *Blackburn v. Alabama* (1960) that a "complex of values
underlies the stricture against use by the state of confessions which,
by way of convenient shorthand, this court terms involuntary, and
the role played by each in any situation varies according to the
particular circumstances of the case" (p. 207). The concept of involuntariness thus represents a summary expression for all practices that
violate constitutional principles (e.g., the right to a fair trial, the
privilege against compulsory self-incrimination) and can be determined only through a comprehensive analysis of the "totality of the
relevant circumstances" (*Culombe v. Connecticut,* 1961, p. 606).
The catalog of factors that may be relevant to a determination of
voluntariness covers a wide range. It includes characteristics of the
accused (e.g., youth, sub-normal intelligence, physical disability,
mental illness, intoxication, illiteracy), the conditions of detention
(e.g., delayed arraignment; inadequate living facilities; lack of access to lawyer, friends, or other assistance), and—of course—the
manner of interrogation (e.g., lengthy, grueling periods of questioning; the use of relays of questioners; multiple interrogators; physical
abuse; deprivation of needs; threats of harm or punishment; advice;
promise or reassurance; and deception). Not surprisingly, the case
law has been confusing and inconsistent, the courts have been bur-
dened by numerous appeals for postconviction reviews of the voluntariness issue, and attempts at synthesis and generalization have met
with little success. As Justice Frankfurter wrote, "there is no simple
litmus-paper test" (*Culombe v. Connecticut,* 1961, p. 601).

As an example of the inconsistency, compare the following rulings: In *Dorsciak v. Gladden* (1967), a confession was *excluded* because the interrogator told the defendant that the judge "would be easier on him." Yet in *People v. Hartgraves* (1964), the confession was *admitted* despite it having followed the interrogator's promise that "it would go easier in court for you if you made a statement."

A HEARING TO ASSESS VOLUNTARINESS

We have noted that voluntariness has emerged as a central concept in determining whether a confession elicited by the police should be admitted into evidence. But how is this implemented?

In one of its clarifying decisions, the Warren Supreme Court, in *Jackson v. Denno* (1964), made explicit the exclusion of those confessions obtained against the will of the accused. In fact, in this case the Court held that criminal defendants have a due-process right that entitles them to a pretrial hearing; its purpose is to determine whether any confessions they have made to officials were voluntarily given and were not the outcome of physical or psychological coercion, which the U.S. Constitution forbids. Only *if* the fact finder—usually the judge, although it could be a jury different from the trial jury—at this coercion hearing determines that a confession was in fact voluntary, may it then be introduced at the jury trial. (Prior to this time, in many states the jury would decide the voluntariness of a confession and hence whether it could be used in deciding guilt or innocence.)

Requiring a judge or some other fact-finding body to screen confessions is a sensible idea, as well as a lifesaving one for some defendants. But that rule did not completely remove the problem. Left unclear in the *Jackson v. Denno* decision was what should be the standard of proof by which the fact finder judges voluntariness. This question came to be a source of controversy. Some states adopted the stringent criterion that voluntariness must be proved *beyond a reasonable doubt*. In contrast, other states approved lesser standards, including proof of voluntariness by a mere *preponderance of the evidence*.[1] The Supreme Court felt it necessary to resolve this discrepancy, but it did not do so until 1972, when conservative appointees had replaced several liberal members of the Supreme Court. In *Lego v. Twomey* (described in Box 2.3) it ruled that only a preponderance of the evidence in the direction of voluntariness was necessary to admit a confession into evidence. Justice Byron White, in the majority opinion, wrote:

> While our decision (in *Jackson v. Denno*) made plain that only voluntary confessions may be admitted at the trial of guilt or innocence, we did not then announce, or even suggest, that the fact-finder at the coercion hearing need judge voluntariness with reference to an especially severe standard of proof. (p. 478)

This decision was clearly a blow for defendants, who would have preferred a more rigorous threshold to be required before such potentially damaging testimony would be introduced to the jurors. (The *Lego* decision did permit any state to adopt a more stringent standard if it so desired.)

In *Lego v. Twomey,* the Supreme Court reasoned that the sole aim of the previous *Jackson v. Denno* decision was to exclude the evidence because it was illegally obtained and hence violated the individual's right to due process, not because of the possible untruthfulness of a coerced confession. In fact, it assumed that jurors can be trusted to use potentially inaccurate confessions cautiously. Specifically, the Court justified the latter position by stating: "Our decision was not based in the slightest on the fear that juries might misjudge the accuracy of confessions and arrive at erroneous determinations of guilt or innocence. . . . Nothing in *Jackson* questioned the province or capacity of juries to assess the truthfulness of confessions" (*Lego v. Twomey,* 1972, p. 485). In Chapter 6 we assess empirically the accuracy of the Court's faith in jurors' capacities and their ability to disregard testimony if they questioned the motives behind it.

THE IMPACT OF THE WARREN COURT

In the 1960s, the Supreme Court moved toward establishing more objective criteria for the admissibility of confession evidence. Up to that point, the refusal of the police to permit the accused to consult with an attorney was regarded as part of the "totality of relevant circumstances" for judging voluntariness. Then in *Massiah v. United States* (1964), the Court ruled that if the accused had been indicted, all incriminating statements elicited by government agents in the absence of counsel were inadmissible. (Winston Massiah was an alleged narcotics dealer who had been released on bail and had hired a lawyer; he was tricked by an informer to make self-incriminating statements about the crime.) The Supreme Court ruled that government actions had breached the Sixth Amendment's provisions that "in all criminal prosecutions, the accused shall enjoy the right . . . to have the assistance of counsel for his defense." In *Escobedo v. Illinois,* also decided in 1964, this principle was extended to include pre-arraignment states of interrogation, and in *Malloy v. Hogan,* also that same year, the Court broadened the exclusionary rule further by explicitly linking confession evidence to the privilege against compulsory self-incrimination.

These decisions culminated in the landmark *Miranda v. Arizona* (1966) decision, in which the Court established broad universally applicable guidelines for safeguarding the rights to counsel and to remain silent. After reviewing the then-contemporary police interrogation techniques, the Supreme Court concluded that they "contain inherently compelling pressures which work to undermine the individual's will to resist" (p. 467) and that "in order to combat these pressures and to permit a full opportunity to exercise the privilege against self-incrimination, the accused must be adequately and effectively apprised of his rights" (p. 467). The Court thus articulated the "Miranda warnings" and ruled that unless the accused is informed of these rights, all self-incriminating statements made are inadmissible.

For almost three decades, the *Miranda* doctrine has stood as the definitive and unambiguous safeguard against confessions that were induced or coerced through interrogation. But in recent years the Court has seen fit to permit erosions of its application; in one case, for example, the Supreme Court decided that "overriding considerations of public safety" could justify a police officer's violation of *Miranda* strictures (*New York v. Quarles,* 1984). One result of this ruling is that, under certain circumstances, a suspect's self-incriminating statements

BOX 2.3
Lego's Confession: Was It Voluntary?

Because the *Lego v. Twomey* decision set in place the lowered standard for admitting confessions into evidence, it is worthwhile to learn the facts of Lego's crime and subsequent interrogation. The following description is taken from the Supreme Court opinion; note that the fact finder is presented with conflicting testimony from the defendant and the police regarding what occurred during interrogation. This is typical.

Petitioner Lego was convicted of armed robbery in 1961 after a jury trial in Superior Court, Cook County, Illinois. The court sentenced him to prison for 25 to 50 years. The evidence introduced against Lego at trial included a confession he had made to police after arrest and while in custody at the station house. Prior to trial Lego sought to have the confession suppressed. He did not deny making it but did challenge that he had done so voluntarily. The trial judge conducted a hearing, out of the presence of the jury, at which Lego testified that police had beaten him about the head and neck with a gun butt. His explanation of this treatment was that the local police chief, a neighbor and former classmate of the robbery victim, had sought revenge upon him. Lego introduced into evidence a photograph that had been taken of him at the county jail on the day after his arrest. This photograph showed that petitioner's face had been swollen and had traces of blood on it. Lego admitted that his face had been scratched in a scuffle with the robbery victim but maintained that the encounter did not explain the condition shown in the photograph. The police chief and four officers also testified. They denied either beating or threatening the petitioner and disclaimed knowledge that any other officer had done so. The trial judge resolved this credibility problem in favor of the police and ruled the confession admissible. At trial, Lego testified on his own behalf. Although he did not dispute the truth of the confession directly, he did tell his version of the events that had transpired at the police station. The trial judge instructed the jury as to the prosecution's burden of proving guilt. He did not instruct that the jury was required to find the confession voluntary before it could be used in judging guilt or innocence. On direct appeal the Illinois Supreme Court affirmed the conviction. (*Lego v. Twomey,* 1972, pp. 480-481)

Thus each statement is self-serving and this becomes a "who-do-you-believe" case. This example reflects our belief that many confessions fit a "gray area"—neither clearly uncoerced nor clearly coerced.

elicited during questioning could be admitted as evidence in a trial even if the suspect had not been apprised of his or her rights. A second result of this public safety exception to *Miranda* is the obvious forfeiture of a clear and objective criterion by which to judge the exclusion of confession evidence. As such, despite calls for the articulation of objective guidelines (White, 1979), in all likelihood the more subjective voluntariness criterion will take on added importance, especially for confessions that will be admitted despite the *Miranda* rule.

In another decision (*Moran v. Burbine,* 1986) that reflects a revisionist interpretation of *Miranda,* the Court has ruled that a suspect undergoing questioning by the police was not entitled to an attorney sent in by his sister, without the suspect's knowledge, as long as he had knowingly waived his right to an attorney. In this particular case, the attorney asked the police if they planned to question the suspect that night, and the police lied to him. The majority opinion of the Supreme Court, although deploring the deliberate falsification, found nothing unconstitutionally improper in the police behavior, as long as the suspect had confessed in full knowledge that he could have had an attorney present if he had wished.

Despite the above relaxations, the majority of the Supreme Court does not necessarily want to eliminate the Miranda warnings completely. Even while upholding the police behavior in the "sister's lawyer" case above, Justice Sandra Day O'Connor wrote in the majority opinion that the *Miranda* rule struck the "proper balance" between society's interests in law enforcement and the protection of defendants' Fifth Amendment rights. And, in a recent decision the Court concluded that once an arrested suspect says he or she wants to talk to an attorney before answering any questions, the police can't question him or her even about an unrelated crime (Taylor, 1988).

A SHIFT TOWARD ADMISSIBILITY

Even though it occurred in 1972, the *Lego v. Twomey* decision was a harbinger of several decisions in the 1990s that signaled a shift toward admissibility to coerced confessions under certain circumstances. [As Justice Brennan wrote in the dissenting opinion to *Lego v. Twomey*, "I do not think it can be denied, given the factual nature of the ordinary voluntariness determination, that permitting a lower standard of proof will necessarily result in the admission of more involuntary confessions than would be admitted were the prosecution required to meet a higher standard" (1972, p. 493).] Because this shift is a radical one, and because we expect it to continue in the future, we devote a separate chapter, Chapter 3, to examining some of these recent decisions in depth.

NOTE

1. Until 1964, there was a third procedure known as the New York rule in which the judge was to exclude a confession as involuntary only if it was not possible that "reasonable men could differ over the inferences to be drawn." Guided by this lax standard, judges would thus admit questionable confessions conditionally and then leave it to the jury to decide both competence and credibility. In *Jackson v. Denno*, the Supreme Court struck down this procedure as a violation of due process. As Justice White stated, "If it finds the confession involuntary, does the jury—indeed, can it—then disregard the confession in accordance with its instruction? . . . These hazards we cannot ignore" (p. 378).

THREE

Recent Court Decisions

A Not-So-Quiet Revolution

SARA L. BLOOM
LAWRENCE S. WRIGHTSMAN

If consistent themes emerged from the Supreme Court decisions of the 1930s through 1960s, they might be that coerced confessions are (a) inherently unfair and (b) of questionable validity. In the past, if—by error—a coerced confession was admitted into evidence and the defendant was found guilty, the defendant's appeal would automatically lead to a reversal of the verdict and a new trial. (An involuntary confession was in the same category as a biased judge or the denial of a defendant's right to attorney—a "structured defect" in the trial process.)

In the past two decades, however, earlier Supreme Court decisions that protected defendants from unfair interrogations and trial procedures have experienced a slow, steady decay (see Box 3.1). The recent and highly publicized "War on Crime" by the federal government has increased the discretion given to the government. One extreme example is a recent Supreme Court decision that involuntary confessions, erroneously admitted at trial, can be deemed harmless if other evidence is strong enough to convict the defendant. A second recent example of the erosion of defendant's rights is evidenced by a recent Supreme Court decision that limits the traditional safeguards on pretrial publicity about a confession. These cases, as well as other recent decisions, will be examined in detail.

The voluntariness of a confession, as noted in Chapter 2, is a legal concept difficult to define. State courts take a different approach in distinguishing between voluntary and involuntary confessions. Whereas a court in one state may determine that a particular confession is voluntary, a court in a different state will often find this same confession involuntary.

Two distinct situations exist in which confessions can be considered involuntary. First, a confession can be deemed involuntary because it was obtained without giving the defendant a *Miranda* warning; this may occur when, during questioning, and while in police custody, a defendant makes incriminating statements but the police fail to inform him or her of the right to remain silent. Second, a confession would also be regarded as involuntary if it were obtained through either physical or psychological coercion by the police.

Such confessions generally will be suppressed before trial. When these inadmissible confessions, however, are improperly admitted at trial and the defendant is convicted, the "harmless error" rule, which will be discussed in detail later in this chapter, is applied. If the appellate court finds the involuntary confession to be "harmless"— that is, the other evidence presented by the prosecution was strong enough to convict without its inclusion—the appellate court will uphold the conviction despite the introduction of an involuntary confession. Nevertheless, confession evidence is so potentially damaging, it is hard to argue that an involuntary confession can ever be considered harmless. Thus, when such confessions are permitted to pollute the process, defendants are deprived of a fair trial. An equally, and therefore, troubling problem is that when police learn that courts do not take a firm stand against coerced confessions, they may be less restrained in conducting investigations.

As noted in Chapter 2, when deciding whether a confession is voluntary, a Court must consider the "totality of the circumstances"; in order words, everything that is possibly relevant to the situation.

Numerous explanations exist for the shift in the direction of the Supreme Court's rulings from the early 1960s to the 1970s and beyond. Fred Graham (1970) notes that at the same time that the Warren Court undertook to limit the powers of the police, the nation began to experience one of its most troubled periods of violent crime and racial unrest. From 1960 to 1968 murders increased by 52%; reported rapes by 84%; robbery by 144%. By the mid-1960s, annual crime reports had registered record increases, and massive ghetto riots were a staple of the mid- and late-1960s. Graham observes: "The Court had announced the most rigid legal limitations that any society had sought to impose on its police at a time when the United States had the most serious crime problem of any so-called advanced nation in the world" (1970, p. 4). By 1965 the Gallup Poll reported that 48% of the public believed that the courts were too lenient with criminal defendants. Three years later, 63% felt that way. Later in 1968, Richard Nixon was elected president, and a shift in the composition of the Court began.

This test is vague and broad, and thus the legal definition of voluntariness is not consistent among the states. The determination of voluntariness is a question of law. As with all matters of law, it is for the judge and not for the jury to decide. As a matter of law, it can be reversed on appeal. Higher courts, however, are often reluctant to overturn such issues on appeal because they do not like to substitute their conclusions for those of the trial judge. For example, in *W. M. v. State* (1991), a Florida court recently questioned whether a confession was voluntary but held that it could not change the ruling made by the trial judge if he or she used the "totality of the circumstances" test.

Three cases will help to illustrate how judges analyze whether a confession is voluntary. The first deals with the confession of a mentally retarded child; the second, a confession by a young man who was lied to by police interrogators; and the third a confession by a mentally disturbed subject. *In each of these cases, the appellate court concluded that the confession was voluntary;* these decisions lead us to question whether the courts have stripped the meaning from the concept of "voluntariness."

In one of these cases, the Supreme Court tightly narrowed the definition of *voluntariness* by holding that to find a confession involuntary, police coercion *must* exist. These cases further support the premise that defendants' rights are deteriorating.

CONFESSION BY A MENTALLY DEFICIENT CHILD

In a recent Florida case, *W. M. v. State* (1991), the appellate court upheld the trial court's conclusion that a confession was voluntary, even though it had been made by a 10-year-old boy with borderline IQ, considered by his teachers as learning disabled, with a demonstrated difficulty in understanding directions. The child had no prior record and had no parent or attorney with him during the 6 hours he was interrogated by the police. Furthermore, evidence existed that the boy was in school or with another officer at some of the times when the alleged burglaries took place. In addition, the child testified that the officers threatened to choke him if he did not confess.

The facts of the case are as follows: At 2:00 p.m. on December 19, 1989, two detectives went to the home of W. M.,[1] a 10-year-old child, and spoke to the child's grandmother. They told the grandmother that they wanted to take W. M. to the police station. The police invited her to come along, but she declined. They also told her that her grandson would not be arrested that day. Before placing the defendant in the police car, one of the police detectives read W. M. his *Miranda* rights from a card. After each right was read, W. M. nodded his head, indicating he understood each right. The detective testified that he did not threaten W. M. At the police station the boy was again advised of his constitutional rights by the police, who read them from a *Miranda* card. The child again nodded his head, and did not request an attorney at any time or invoke his right to remain silent. W. M. was brought into a room and was given a soft drink and some candy, after which he allegedly confessed to having committed the burglaries.

The next day, after another detective read W. M. his rights, W. M. told him that he committed other burglaries. The child was then arrested and taken to the Division of Youth Services—Detention Center. There were no written acknowledgments by any of the detectives that the warnings were given, either verbally or in writing. No tape recordings or notes were made of any of the interrogation sessions, and no parent or guardian attended any of the interviews. The court stated that the failure to have a waiver in writing did not invalidate the statement. Further, according to the police, no threats were made against the child and the conditions surrounding the statements in the police station were not coercive. The majority of the Court asserted that the prosecution bears a heavy burden in establishing that a defendant's waiver of his *Miranda* rights was intelligently made. The prosecutor, however, need only establish by a preponderance of the evidence the voluntariness of a *Miranda* waiver (see the *Lego v. Twomey* decision in Chapter 2).

In conclusion, a majority of the Florida appellate court did not find that the trial judge erred in denying the defendant's motion to suppress the confession and, therefore, the defendant's conviction was allowed to stand. The appellate judges stated that the admissibility of a confession depends not only on the defendant's age but on his intelligence, education, experience, and the ability to comprehend the meaning and effect of his statement. The judge said that he was arrested, although not convicted, one year before, and therefore understood the process and his rights. At this prior arrest, however, he was never questioned and did not invoke any of his rights. The majority of the court believed that W. M. voluntarily, knowingly, and intelligently waived his *Miranda* rights and voluntarily told the detectives that he committed the burglaries. Further, the majority of the court did not believe the boy's testimony about how the officers threatened to hang him by his neck if he did not confess.

In a dissenting opinion, a minority of the Florida appellate court stated that "properly sifted, the evidence shows that it was likely the product of a very frightened little boy who, under the circumstances, probably would have confessed to anything to get out of there."

Without the confession, the child probably would not have been convicted. The record does not state any other evidence linking the defendant with the crime. In fact, there is evidence to the contrary.[2]

CONFESSION UNDER
EXTENUATING CIRCUMSTANCES

In a 1990 California case (*People v. Thompson*) the court found a confession voluntary even though the police told the defendant that if he made a statement he could exonerate his pregnant girlfriend and have her released from custody. Defendant Robert Jackson Thompson was convicted of the first degree murder of 12-year-old Benjamin Brenneman. He also was convicted of forcible sodomy, lewd conduct with a child under the age of 14, and felony child endangerment.

When Benjamin Brenneman did not return home after his paper route, the police were contacted to investigate. They found his bicycle near the building where the defendant lived. One tenant mentioned that she had seen the defendant talking with the victim, so police went to his apartment, but he was not home. The defendant arrived at his apartment at 1:00 in the morning. He told the police that the victim went to his apartment to get him to subscribe to the newspaper. The police asked if they could search the apartment and they found a pair of sandals, later found to be Benjamin Brenneman's. The defendant first said that they were his girlfriend's, but then said that he found them in the hallway. He also said that the victim never entered his apartment, but when the officers started talking about checking for fingerprints in the apartment, he said the victim entered when he was looking for money. He stated that after the victim left, he went to Huntington Beach to pick up a woman, because he was tired of sex every night with Lisa, his girlfriend, but had not found one. He said that he lived with Lisa and was happy with her, but wanted to have sex with other women. He also told the officers that on the way back the muffler fell off his car, and he spent an hour fixing it. When the officers examined the car, the muffler was firmly in place. They asked the defendant to contact them the next day at noon and left the defendant's apartment.

The next day Ben's body was found at the base of a road embankment in a rural area. He was bound in ropes; one rope was looped tightly around his neck four times. Medical experts testified that Ben was strangled to death. In addition, sperm was found in his anus.

The defendant contacted the detectives at noon as promised and drove with them to the area where the defendant said he had been during Ben's disappearance. The police took soil samples from that area and told the defendant that they could compare it with soil on the defendant's tire to determine if he was really in that area. After they went back to the police station, one of the detectives asked the defendant to contact him the next day at 4:00 p.m. The defendant left and drove back to the place he said he was at the night before, and pulled his car off onto the dirt. He made a U-turn and drove back to his apartment.

The defendant failed to contact the police at 4:00 p.m., and was found and arrested at a shopping mall and taken into custody. When he learned that his girlfriend was ill, and might have a miscarriage, he asked to speak with the detective. He was interrogated for several hours and admitted to committing lewd acts with the victim, but denied killing the boy. According to the court opinion the conversation went as follows:

> Defendant spoke of his love for Lisa and started to cry. Tuttle left to get coffee and Kleenex. When he returned he said to defendant, "the thing is, Bobby, you know, I'm not totally convinced that she doesn't know something about this . . . I'll have to present the case to . . . the D.A.'s office and it's going to be up to them to make the determination as to whether or not she stays. . . . Information hasn't come forward at this time which would cause me to release her. See what I'm saying?"
>
> A few minutes later, Tuttle said to the defendant, "I think if you truly loved her, you wouldn't allow her to sit here in jail if you knew information that would help her. See what I'm saying? . . . If the D.A.'s decide to prosecute and she's found guilty, . . . that could really push her over the edge. I'm not saying it will, Bobby, I'm just, you know, I think we should explore all possibilities. . . . You're what's important to her more than anything in the world right now. And I think . . . if she is incarcerated . . . it

could really break her. Up to this point, I don't really have any reason . . . to release her. Like I told you before . . . unless something else comes forward that can show that she's totally uninvolved. You know what I'm saying?"

The defendant responded, "I was told by the Public Defender . . . not to talk at all . . . I don't even think I should be talking now . . . ." The conversation, however, continued. After Detective Tuttle reminded the defendant that the victim's body was found in Palos Verdes, he said, "We got a nice plaster cast of your front tires over there. How do you explain that?" The police did not have plaster casts, and at that time did not have evidence to connect the defendant with the site where the body was found.

The defendant denied going to Palos Verdes, and continued to declare that he was not a killer. Tuttle then inquired, "what if there's another side . . . to Robert Thompson?" The defendant responded, "I don't know. I don't think there is . . . If there is, God help me. Please, help me . . . if there is. Because I love Lisa. . . . And if there's another side to me, help me." Tuttle asked if there was a chance that he sometimes blacked out and did not remember what he did. Thompson said, "Yes, there is . . . I'm scared at those times." They went over what the defendant did on the night of the murder, but this time he said he had been drunk and did not remember anything. Tuttle asked the defendant if he might have committed the crime and forgotten it; the defendant said, "I don't think I did." Then Tuttle asked him to assume that he had done it, and explain how it happened, but the defendant refused.

Officer Johnson took over the interrogation. After questioning the defendant over a variety of topics, Johnson proclaimed, "I don't believe in bullshitting around and also I'm gonna tell you the way it is." He then told the defendant that his car was linked to the place where the body was found, and that a blue trunk found in the back of his car contained physical evidence linking it to the victim. Neither of these assertions were true. Officer Johnson then stated that he believed the defendant had tied the victim as part of a sexual trip and killed him unintentionally.

Officer Johnson and the defendant started talking about when the boy arrived at the defendant's apartment. The defendant admitted that the victim had brought the newspaper found in the apartment. Johnson declared, falsely, that the police obtained rope fibers found in the defendant's bedroom and, said truthfully, that a witness had seen the defendant carrying the trunk out of the apartment the evening of the crime. Johnson concluded that while he thought the defendant killed the victim unintentionally, "We'll see you in court, and I can tell you we're going with the . . . theory right now that you killed him so you wouldn't get identified. . . . You remember everything you do, the only question is whether you want to talk about it, and it's obvious that you don't want to talk about it. So I'm wasting my time."

The defendant, however, immediately said he wanted to carry on with the conversation. At this point Tuttle returned to the room and showed Thompson a photograph of the body. Johnson again reviewed the claimed evidence, true and false, against the defendant. He asserted that if the defendant did not talk, the police would proceed on the theory of an intentional killing, and then he left the room.

Tuttle turned to the defendant and asked, "Why did you do it?" Thompson, fearing that he was being recorded, asked Tuttle to talk to him in the hall. In the hall, the defendant began crying, "I didn't mean to do it. When I left him, he was alive." Tuttle described the defendant's appearance: "He was crying profusely. He was shaking. He was having a hard time supporting himself on his feet. He was being assisted by Detective Johnson and myself."

The detectives and the defendant went back into the interrogation room, where the defendant said that he proposed a sexual act to the victim and touched him. He also admitted leaving the body tied up in the road. Defendant continued to insist that the victim was alive when defendant left him. (*People v. Thompson,* 1990, pp. 159-163)

At the trial the defense presented evidence from several witnesses. One neighbor said that the boy came to her door to solicit a newspaper subscription, and that she saw a man, who was not the defendant, invite the victim to go with him and play pool. A clerk at a billiards parlor testified that he saw the victim and a man other than the defendant at his establishment between 10:00 p.m. and 10:30 p.m.

The defendant testified that he had been drinking that day and put his arm around the victim and asked him if he would like to have a sexual relationship. The victim said no and then left the apartment. The defendant said that he initially lied to the police because he was afraid that he would get in trouble due to the fact that he made sexual advances toward the victim. The defendant testified that the reason why he talked with Detective Tuttle in jail was because he thought that if he said something, his girlfriend would be released from custody. He came to believe, however, that because of what the officers said to him about his "darker side" and all the evidence against him, he had taken and bound the boy, but somehow suppressed the memory.

After the jury unanimously voted to convict the defendant, the jurors were asked to recommend a sentence. Nine out of the 12 jurors voted for the death penalty. Due to the split vote, the judge declared a mistrial and ordered a new sentencing trial. During retrial, the prosecution offered evidence regarding the defendant's prior record. The prosecutor called the victim of a prior conviction, who testified that in 1978 the defendant had forced him to engage in acts of sodomy and oral copulation. The prosecutor also introduced into evidence documentary proof of the defendant's 1967 conviction for child molestation.

At that point, the jury unanimously voted for the death penalty. On appeal the defense argued that the defendant's statements made during the conversations with the detectives were inadmissible. The defense appeal claimed that psychological coercion overcame the defendant's will to resist and brought about confessions not freely self-determined. To support this contention, the defense stated that the police repeatedly lied to Thompson in an attempt to convince him that further denial of guilt was hopeless. The officers falsely told the defendant that his car had been connected with the scene of the boy's death by tire tracks and soil samples, that they had found physical evidence linked to the victim in the defendant's car and the trunk, and that they had found rope fibers in the defendant's bedroom.

The defense also argued that regardless of the defendant's girlfriend's medical problems, she would only be released if the defendant would discuss the crime with the detective. The defense used *People v. Trout,* a 1960 California case, to support this position. In this case, the court held a confession to be involuntary when police indicated to the defendant, Trout, that if he confessed, his wife would be released to take care of their children.

The prosecution cited two earlier California cases in response to *Trout,* claiming that they were analogous to the Thompson case. It stated that in one of these as in the *Thompson* case, the defendant's wife was taken into custody because she was living with the defendant. The officer told the defendant that if the defendant told the truth and there was no evidence to hold his wife, she would be released. The court observed that the officers made it clear to the defendant that the defendant's wife would not be prosecuted if no evidence of her guilt was procured, but this was not a threat to prosecute her if the defendant did not confess the crime nor a promise to release her if he did. In the earlier case, the court ruled that even if the principal motive for a confession was that it would probably result in the exoneration of another person who was suspected of complicity in the offense, such a fact does not render the confession involuntary.

In responding to Thompson's appeal, the California Supreme Court held that deception does not necessarily invalidate a confession. The court did, however, say that it is a factor in finding a confession voluntary or not. It mentioned a court case, *In re Walker,* a 1974 case, that held a confession voluntary because "the deception was not of a type reasonably likely to procure an untrue statement." In this case, the defendant on his way to the hospital was deceptively told that he should talk because he would probably soon die. The court also referred to *People v. Watkins,* a 1970 case, in which officers falsely told the defendant that his fingerprints were found on the getaway car.

Furthermore, the court stated that there is a fine line between what is a threat or promise and a statement of fact or intention. The court found that Thompson voluntarily made the statements to the detectives. They supported their finding on the following: The tone of the interrogation was restrained and noncoercive, the defendant did not mention his girlfriend when he and the detective went out into the hall, and the defendant did not request to discontinue the conversation. The court stated that in California and prior to the enactment of Article 1, section 28, of the California Constitution, the prosecution must prove voluntariness beyond a reasonable doubt. Even with that very high standard of proof, the court found the defendant's incriminating statements properly admitted into evidence. In a footnote, the court stated that the defendant's statements were vital in the prosecution's case. The court said that without them the prosecution would only have circumstantial evidence that might not persuade a jury that the defendant was guilty beyond a reasonable doubt, and would probably require reversal of the conviction.

POLICE COERCION NEEDED TO FIND
A CONFESSION INVOLUNTARY

Courts have a difficult time concluding that a confession is involuntary when there is no instigation by the police to confess. Therefore, a dilemma may arise when a mentally ill or highly intoxicated person confesses. In 1986, in *Colorado v. Connelly,* the U.S. Supreme Court dealt with this situation. In the end, the majority of the court held a confession voluntary because the police complied with *Miranda,*[3] although the defendant, at the time he confessed, was hearing voices telling him to confess. The majority also held that the state is required to prove there was a *Miranda* waiver only by a preponderance of the evidence, and that the waiver is to be determined involuntary under the Fifth Amendment only if police coercion is involved.

On August 18, 1983, the defendant, Francis Connelly, walked over to Officer Patrick Anderson of the Denver Police Department and told him that he murdered someone and wanted to talk about it. The police officer immediately read Connelly his rights. Connelly said he understood his rights, but wanted to talk about the murder anyway. He also told the officer that he had been institutionalized in five different mental institutions. Soon after, Homicide Detective Antuna arrived on the scene. Connelly told them that he returned all the way from Boston to confess that he murdered Mary Ann Junta, a young girl who had been killed in Denver in November 1982. The defendant took them to the location of the crime. The detectives testified that they did not perceive that Connelly was suffering a mental illness. Connelly was held overnight.

The next day when a public defender talked with Connelly, he became visibly disoriented. He gave confusing answers, and stated that he followed "voices" that told him to come to Denver and confess. At this point, authorities sent him to a state hospital for a psychiatric evaluation. He was initially found incompetent to assist in his own defense, but by March 1984 doctors felt he was competent to go to trial.

A psychiatrist employed by the state hospital testified that the defendant was suffering from chronic schizophrenia and was in a psychotic state at least as of August 17, 1983, the day before he confessed.[4] The psychiatrist said he could not make free and rational choices, because he was experiencing command hallucinations; he further testified that Connelly's cognitive abilities were not significantly impaired, and therefore he understood the *Miranda* rights given to him by the detective. The psychiatrist conceded that the "voices" could in reality be Connelly's interpretation of his own guilt, but said he truly believed that it was Connelly's psychosis that motivated his confession.

The trial judge found the statements involuntary (even though the police did nothing wrong or coercive) in that Connelly's mental illness destroyed his free will. The trial court based its decision on two U.S. Supreme Court cases, *Townsend v. Sain,* 1963, and *Culombe v. Connecticut,* 1961, that held that a confession is admissible only if it is a product of the defendant's rational intellect and "free will."

The Colorado Supreme Court affirmed this decision, and stated that "one's capacity for rational judgment and free choice may be overborne as much by certain forms of severe mental illness as by external pressure."

The U.S. Supreme Court, however, reversed the Colorado Supreme Court's decision. It held that *coercive police activity is necessary* to find a confession not "voluntary" within the meaning of the Due Process Clause of the Fourteenth Amendment. Because the police did not coerce the defendant in obtaining the confession, the Court found no basis for concluding that any agent of the state has deprived the defendant of due process of law. The Supreme Court distinguished this case from *Blackburn v. Alabama* (1960) and *Townsend v. Sain* in which the court held that the "deficient mental condition of the defendants in those cases was sufficient to render their confessions involuntary." In those cases, unlike *Connelly*, police acted unjustly, said the Supreme Court.[5]

In addition, the Supreme Court ruled that the Colorado Supreme Court had used the wrong standard in determining whether there was a voluntary *Miranda* waiver. The Supreme Court has long held that the State has a heavy burden of proving that a *Miranda* waiver exists, but the majority stated that the Colorado Supreme Court should have used a lower standard, the "preponderance of evidence" standard, rather than using a "clear and convincing" standard.[6] The majority also disagreed with the Colorado Supreme Court's ruling that the defendant's waiver was involuntary because it was made not of his own free will. The majority of the Supreme Court responded,

> the sole concern of the Fifth Amendment, upon which *Miranda* was based, is governmental coercion; Fifth Amendment privilege is not concerned with moral and psychological pressures to confess emanating from sources other than official coercion. Voluntariness of waiver of right to remain silent depends upon absence of police overreaching, not on "free choice" in any broader sense of the word." (*Colorado v. Connelly*, 1986, p. 170)[7]

Justices Brennan and Marshall strongly dissented to Chief Justice Rehnquist's majority opinion in the *Connelly* case because they believed that "the use of a mentally ill person's involuntary confession is antithetical to the notion of fundamental fairness embodied in the Due Process Clause." In their dissent they argued,

> The absence of police wrongdoing should not, by itself, determine the voluntariness of a confession by a mentally ill person. The requirement that a confession be voluntary reflects a recognition of the importance of free will and of reliability in determining the admissibility of a confession, and thus demands an inquiry into the totality of the circumstances surrounding the confession. . . . Until today, we have never upheld the admission of a confession that does not reflect the exercise of free will. (*Colorado v. Connelly*, 1986, p. 176)

The dissenting justices also argued that the preponderance of the evidence standard is too low, the waiver of *Miranda* was not voluntary, and that state action did exist. As to the existence of state action and whether the confession was voluntary, the dissent stated in a footnote that even if police knowledge of the defendant's mental illness was required to exclude an involuntary confession (see *Townsend v. Sain,* 1963), the record supports a conclusion of awareness by the police. This finding is based on the following: Shortly after the defendant approached Officer Anderson, the defendant told him that he had been a patient in several mental hospitals; Officer Anderson stated that his first thought of Connelly was that the defendant was a "crackpot," and Officer Anderson informed Detective Antuna about the defendant's institutionalizations. Because of these facts, it was hard for the dissenting justices to believe that the officers could not detect that the defendant was suffering from a mental illness.

Even though it is recognized that mental illness often plays a big part in determining whether a defendant's statements are voluntary, *Connelly* limits this factor, by holding that for a confession to violate the Due Process Clause of the Fourteenth Amendment, police coercion must be present. The question for lower courts under these circumstances is: What constitutes police coercion? Is knowledge by the police that the defendant is mentally ill enough? Probably not. The majority of *Connelly* states that even when a causal connection exists between police misconduct and the defendant's confession, a violation of due process is not automatic.

The holding in *Connelly* has also been applied to cases where the defendant has given a confession under the heavy influence of drugs or alcohol. For example, an Illinois appellate court in 1988 held that because there was no police coercion, it did not have to consider the general rule of whether the defendant's will was overwhelmed by the effects of the medication. Although not specifically stated in the record, it is assumed that the reason why the defendant contended that he did not voluntarily confess was because he was highly medicated and not aware of what was going on.

The defendant confessed while in critical condition in the intensive care unit within 12 hours after being shot twice and within 3 to

4 hours of receiving doses of Demerol and Valium. The court found no police coercion because of the following: The defendant's doctor gave permission to question the defendant and told the detective and the State Attorney that the defendant knew what was happening; the attorney read the defendant his *Miranda* rights and provided a sheet containing the warnings; and the detective and attorney did not notice any mental deficiencies resulting from the medication and the defendant read and corrected his statement. Was *Connelly* properly applied in this case? Was there police coercion?

Although lower courts apply *Connelly* in different contexts, many courts today assume or find that sufficient state action is present. The "totality of the circumstances test," therefore, is used in deciding whether the confession was voluntary. As we have previously discussed, this test is quite subjective. Despite their reluctance to disturb findings of the trial court, in some instances judges on a higher court will reverse the trial court's finding on this issue. When this occurs the "harmless error" rule, discussed in the following paragraphs, applies.

APPLYING THE "HARMLESS ERROR" RULE TO CONFESSIONS

Always in the past, when a confession was introduced into evidence and on appeal the appellate court believed that the confession should not have been admitted, the case had to be retried. But in 1991 the U.S. Supreme Court in *Arizona v. Fulminante* overturned previous case law and held that a conviction can stand even if the confession admitted as evidence in the case is involuntary or coerced as long as the confession is deemed "harmless." A confession is deemed harmless if the state can demonstrate that the admission of the confession did not contribute to the conviction. In this case, the U.S. Supreme Court asserted that the confession was coerced and *not* harmless, but it went on to make a ruling applicable to *other* instances in which the error *was* harmless.

The *Fulminante* case involves a defendant charged with the murder of his 11-year-old stepdaughter. On September 14, 1982, Oreste

Fulminante called the Mesa, AZ, Police Department, to report his stepdaughter, Jeneane Hunt, missing. Jeneane's mother was in the hospital and during this time Oreste was caring for the child. Two days later the body was found in the desert east of Mesa. She had been shot twice in the head at close range with a large weapon. Officials could not tell whether or not she had been sexually assaulted, because her body was severely decomposed.

Fulminante told the police many inconsistent stories regarding Jeneane's disappearance and his relationship with her; at times he blamed the child for problems in the family's relationship. In effect, he became a suspect in her killing. When charges were not filed against him, he left for New Jersey. There, he was charged and convicted of possession of a firearm by a felon, and was sent to a federal prison in New York; while there he met Anthony Sarivola, former police officer and a fellow inmate who was a paid informant for the Federal Bureau of Investigation.[8] Sarivola masqueraded as an organized crime figure.

Fulminante became friends with Sarivola, and Sarivola heard that Fulminante was suspected of murdering a child and brought up the topic numerous times. Each time Fulminante denied any involvement in Jeneane's death. The defendant once told him that bikers who were looking for drugs killed her, and another time he told him that he did not know what had happened. Sarivola told the defendant that he knew that other inmates were giving him a hard time because they believed that he was a child molester and murderer. He offered to protect Fulminante if Fulminante told him the truth about the murder.[9] Sarivola testified that the defendant told him that he had driven Jeneane to the desert on his motorcycle, where he choked her, sexually assaulted her, and made her beg for her life, before shooting her twice in the head.

After being released from prison, Fulminante 6 months later allegedly described in detail to Mrs. Sarivola how he brutally killed his stepdaughter. Mrs. Sarivola testified that she was appalled by his statements, but took a trip with him anyway, and did not contact the authorities.[10]

In the District Court of Arizona, the court held that the confession was voluntary and was therefore properly admitted into evidence.

The jury found Fulminante guilty as charged, and the judge sentenced the defendant to death. The case was appealed, but the Supreme Court of Arizona affirmed the trial court's decision and held that the harmless error rule applied. It held that although the first confession was coerced, it was harmless, in part because there was a second confession. At the same time, the second confession was not tainted by the first confession, because it was made 6 months after the first. Upon Fulminante's motion for reconsideration, however, the Supreme Court of Arizona ruled that the U.S. Supreme Court's precedent did *not* allow the use of the harmless error analysis in the case of a coerced confession. It reversed the conviction and remanded the case back to trial court to decide the case without the first confession, which it concluded had been made under the pressure of a plausible threat of violence.

The majority of the U.S. Supreme Court affirmed the Supreme Court of Arizona's holding, but overturned the District Court conviction on different reasoning. It held for the first time that an involuntary or coerced confession *is* subject to the harmless error rule. Prior to this ruling, the Court held that admitting a coerced confession into evidence over objection violated the Due Process Clause of the Fourteenth Amendment, and that because a coerced confession is fundamentally different from other types of erroneously admitted evidence to which the harmless error rule has been applied, it could never be harmless.

According to *Chapman v. California,* prior cases "have indicated that there are some constitutional rights so basic to a fair trial that their infraction can never be treated as "harmless error" (1967, p. 23). The constitutional rule against using a defendant's coerced confession against him at this criminal trial was included in that category. In *Lego v. Twomey,* the court said that using a defendant's coerced confession against him is a denial of due process of law regardless of the other evidence in the record aside from the confession, even when another confession of the defendant had been properly admitted into evidence (1972, p. 483).

Also, in *Payne v. Arkansas,* the Court said, "[When] a coerced confession constitutes a part of the evidence before the jury and a general verdict is returned, no one can say what credit and weight the jury gave to the confession" (1958, p. 568). Therefore, no confession can be deemed harmless, just as a biased judge or the deprivation of counsel is never harmless. Justice White, in *Cruz v. New York*, on behalf of the dissent, stated, "[A defendant's confession] is probably the most probative and damaging evidence that can be admitted against him" (1987, p. 195). It is "so damaging that a jury should not be expected to ignore it even if told to do so" (*Bruton v. United States*, 1968, p. 140). The court in *Chambers v. Florida* (1940) even went so far to say that "permitting a coerced confession to be part of the evidence on which a jury is free to base its verdict of guilty is inconsistent with the thesis that ours is not an inquisitional system of criminal justice" (pp. 235-236).

Justice White, on behalf of Justices Marshall, Blackmun, and Stevens, made the strong statement in the *Fulminante* (1991) minority opinion that "the majority of the Court, without any justification, overrules this vast body of precedent without a word and in so doing dislodges one of the fundamental tenets of our criminal justice system" (p. 1254).

In this particular case, however, the confessions inadmissibly used at trial were not harmless. Justice White gave several reasons why the State had failed to meet its burden that the confession was harmless beyond a reasonable doubt. First, he stated that a successful prosecution depended on the jury believing both confessions, because other evidence was weak. In addition, the confession to Mrs. Sarivola could have depended on the first confession, and therefore, the two confessions corroborated each other. Without the first confession, the jurors might not have believed the wife's story because she was given favorable treatment for herself and her husband.

PRETRIAL PUBLICITY ABOUT A CONFESSION

Another Supreme Court decision that has an effect on the outcome of cases that involve confessions is *Mu'Min v. Virginia* (1991). This case held that a defendant's Sixth Amendment right to an impartial jury and his Fourteenth Amendment right to due process were not violated when the trial judge on voir dire refused to question prospective jurors about specific contents of news reports to which they had been exposed. In effect, if an attorney cannot find out whether a juror has been exposed through the media that the defendant confessed to the crime, and a juror has been exposed to such information, then jurors may unjustly convict the defendant on this information even if they say that they will only consider the evidence before them.

The case involved a Virginia inmate, Dawud Majid Mu'Min, serving time for first-degree murder, who was convicted of murdering Gladys Nopwasky while out of prison on work detail. On September 22, 1988, Gladys Nopwasky was stabbed to death in her retail carpet and flooring store in Dale City, VA. Because of the gross negligence on the part of the corrections officers, the case generated a great deal of publicity in the local news media. The trial judge denied the defendant's motion for individual questioning of prospective jurors; furthermore, the judge rejected questions to prospective jurors about what they had specifically seen, read, or heard about the case, or from what or whom they had obtained their knowledge of the case (Dicks, 1992). The judge asked the group of prospective jurors only whether they were exposed to news reports involving the defendant. One juror admitted to having formed an opinion as to the defendant's guilt; he was excused for cause. Then the judge asked the jurors in groups of four if they formed an opinion as to the guilt of the defendant. One juror was not sure she could be impartial and was excused by the judge, and several others were excused for various reasons. Eight of the 12 eventual jurors, however, admitted that they had read or heard something about the case. They did not indicate that they had formed an opinion based on the outside information or would be biased in any way, but virtually all the information published prior to the trial favored the prosecution.

Some of the 47 articles that talked about the case explained the murder and investigation in detail. Under the banner headlines, "Mu'Min Confessed to Killing Gladys Nopwasky" and "Inmate Said to Admit to Killing," the press included the news of Mu'Min's indictment with the proud announcement of Virginia's Secretary of Transportation and Public Safety that the State had already secured Mu'Min's acknowledgment of responsibility for the murder. Subsequent stories reported that, upon being confronted with the charges, Mu'Min initially offered the incredible claim that he had entered the store only to help Nopwasky after witnessing another man attempting to rape her. According to these reports, however, Mu'Min eventually abandoned this story and confessed to having stabbed Nopwasky twice with a steel spike. One of these stories was carried under the front-page headline: "Accused Killer Says He Stabbed Dale City Woman After Argument."

Newspaper accounts also described the following: Mu'Min's prior crime; "his background, including nearly two dozen violations of prison rules and six denials of parole, prior meandering from the work detail and criminal activities while out, and statements by fellow inmates about his 'strange' behavior" (Dicks, 1992, p. 1). All this occurred at the same time that the Willie Horton case was an issue in the 1988 election campaign. Not surprisingly, the jury found Mu'Min guilty of capital murder, and recommended that he be executed.

As we noted, when Mu'Min appealed his conviction, based on the judge's refusal to allow the specific voir dire questions, the Supreme Court upheld the judge's refusal. The Supreme Court noted, however, that a trial court's findings of juror impartiality may "be overturned only for 'manifest error.' " In *Patton v. Yount* (1984) the Supreme Court held that "adverse pretrial publicity can create such a presumption of prejudice in a community that the jurors' claims that they can be impartial should not be believed." An example is found in *Irvin v. Dowd* (1961). In this case news reports included details of the defendant's confessions to 24 burglaries and six murders, including the one for which he was tried, as well as his unacceptable offer to plead guilty in order to avoid the death sentence. They contained numerous opinions as to his guilt, as well as opinions about the appropriate punishment. The dissent, however, stated that Mu'Min did not argue that the pretrial publicity was extensive enough to create a presumption of community prejudice, but that the publicity was prejudicial enough to create a presumption of prejudice on the part of any individual juror who actually read it.

The majority of the Supreme Court in this opinion stated that this case is different because the reports about Mu'Min did not contain the same sort of damaging information; no "wave of public passion" equivalent to the *Irvin* situation existed. Publicity was more focused on the incompetency on the part of the Department of Corrections.

Justices Marshall, Blackmun, and Stevens dissented. They stated that this decision "turns a critical constitutional guarantee—the Sixth Amendment's right to an impartial jury—into a hollow formality." (*Mu'Min v. Virginia*, 1991, p. 1909). Their vigorous dissent stated that when a prospective juror has been exposed to prejudicial pretrial publicity, a trial court cannot realistically assess the juror's impartiality without first establishing what the juror already has learned about the case (p. 1910). The dissent also stated that once a prospective juror admits exposure to pretrial publicity, "content" questioning must be part of the voir dire for at least three reasons. First, "content" questioning is necessary to determine whether the type and extent of the publicity to which a prospective juror has been exposed would disqualify the juror as a matter of law. Our system of justice recognizes that, under certain circumstances, exposure to particularly inflammatory publicity creates so strong a presumption of prejudice that "the jurors' claims that they can be impartial should not be believed" (*Patton v. Yount*, 1984, p. 1033).

Second, even when pretrial publicity is not so extreme as to disqualify prospective jurors who have been exposed to it, content questioning still is essential to give legal depth to the trial court's finding of impartiality. One of the reasons that a "juror may be unaware of" his own bias is that the issue of impartiality is a mixed question of law and fact, the resolution of which necessarily draws upon the trial court's legal expertise. Where, as in this case, a trial judge asks a prospective juror merely whether he can be "impartial," the judge may well get an answer that is the product of the juror's own confusion as to what impartiality is. By asking the prospective juror—in addition—to identify what he or she has read or heard about the case and what corresponding impressions the juror has formed, the trial judge is able to confirm that "the impartiality that the juror professes is the same impartiality that the Sixth Amendment demands" (*Mu'Min v. Virginia*, 1991, p. 1914).

The third reason that Justice Marshall gave in his dissent was that "content" questioning facilitates accurate trial court fact-finding. As this Supreme Court has recognized, the impartiality "determination is essentially one of credibility." Where a prospective juror acknowledges exposure to pretrial publicity, the precise content of that publicity constitutes contextual information essential to an accurate assessment of whether the prospective juror's profession of impartiality is believable. If the trial judge declines to develop this background, its finding of impartiality simply does not merit appellate deference to the trial judge's decision. Justice Marshall believed that two of the newspaper stories were so prejudicial that any juror exposed to them should have automatically been excused. Justice Kennedy also dissented. He believed that the questions asked of the prospective jurors in this case were deficient in that the jurors could simply remain silent as an implied indication of a lack of bias or prejudice. The trial court could thereby not assess the credibility of the individuals seated on this jury. He stated that the "trial judge should have substantial discretion in conducting the voir dire, but findings of impartiality must be based on something more than the mere silence of the individual in response to questions asked en masse" [*Mu'Min v. Virginia,* p. 1919 (Justice Kennedy, dissenting)].

CONCLUSION

These Supreme Court decisions, particularly those in the Fulminante and Mu'Min appeals, are not simply reversals of previous Court decisions. They are more than that. They raise the likelihood that previously resolved issues can now resurface, to be dealt with on a case-by-case basis. A tangible benefit of the *Miranda* rule was to make explicit the exclusion of involuntary confessions. Now, police may be tempted to exceed the *Miranda* guidelines because a coercive interrogation leading to a forced confession may be ruled "harmless" if other evidence (perhaps indirectly produced as a result of the interrogation) is enough to convict the defendant. Or prosecutors may interject evidence from "questionable confessions in borderline cases in the hope that any resulting confession will be upheld" (Lacayo, 1991, p. 26). In the concluding chapter of this book we attempt to assess whether this is happening.

NOTES

1. Because the identity of juveniles is protected under the law, courts refer to juveniles by their initials rather than their full names.

2. In *State v. Cervantes* (1991) an appellate court held, in a cocaine-possession case, that a confession was anything but harmless when, without the confession, the prosecution proved only that the defendant was present at the house and had a key to its garage.

3. Note that *Miranda* applies in this case because the custody requirement was satisfied, because the officers handcuffed the defendant.

4. Before Mr. Connelly confessed, he had been committed five times suffering from chronic paranoid schizophrenia. He was once hospitalized for 7 months. He heard imaginary voices and saw nonexistent objects. He believed that his father was God, and that he was a reincarnation of Jesus.

5. The dissent stated that in *Townsend,* the police "wrongdoing" only consisted of the police physician *allegedly* giving the defendant a drug with truth-serum properties, and that the officers who obtained the confession knew that the defendant had been given drugs, but did not know the type of drugs given. The police wrongdoing was not an essential factor in determining voluntariness, according to the court.

6. The Supreme Court stated that although they narrowed the standard, the Colorado legislature can broaden these rights statutorily through its rules of evidence.

7. Although the majority holds that police coercion is necessary for a *Miranda* waiver to be involuntary, it does not state that police coercion is necessary as to the question of whether the defendant knowingly and intelligently waived *Miranda*. In effect, lower courts have inconsistently interpreted *Connelly* as to this issue. For example, in *United States v. Bradshaw* (1988), a U.S. Court of Appeals case, the court reversed the lower court on this issue and held that although police coercion is a necessary prerequisite to determining that a *Miranda* waiver was involuntary, it did not have any bearing on the separate question of whether the defendant was too mentally ill to understand *Miranda* warnings so as to make a knowing and intelligent waiver.

8. As we saw in *Connelly,* a confession to be considered a constitutional issue must have been obtained through state action. Because the informant was "working" for the FBI, this requirement was satisfied. If the defendant confessed to a friend, and the police, FBI, or other state or federal agency was not involved, then the defendant could not argue that it was unconstitutionally obtained.

9. Mr. Sarivola said to the defendant, "You have to tell me about it . . . for me to give you any help."

10. Mr. and Mrs. Sarivola were placed in the Federal Witness Protection Program. Furthermore, Mr. Sarivola previously fabricated a tape recording in connection with an earlier, unrelated FBI investigation.

11. The court held that the defendant's confession made within 5 hours after he had been beaten by police and threatened with death, was involuntary, and the defendant's second confession, made 10 hours after he was beaten by police and threatened with death, was also involuntary.

F O U R

Police Interrogations

Some confessions gush forth spontaneously; others emerge, as we saw in the Fulminante case in Chapter 3, in conversations between prisoners who share a jail cell. But typically a confession is given to the police, during the questioning of a suspect. What is the role of interrogations in generating confessions? Do police have a standard procedure for questioning suspects? Are certain techniques considered unacceptable, even if they might be admissible in court? One of the purposes of this chapter is to examine police interrogation procedures currently in use in the United States. But the other purpose is to review the use of interrogation as a device to generate confessions throughout history, and in other countries.

A HISTORICAL REVIEW OF THE USE OF CONFESSIONS

Every society has been concerned with violations of its laws, customs, and social expectations. Those who were suspected of such violations were often subjected to interrogation in hopes that they would confess. Many did.

Franklin (1970) noted that the first pictures ever drawn of police— found in Twelfth Dynasty Egyptian tombs of about 2000 B.C.—show them administering the third degree to a suspect. In light of the video-tape of Rodney King's arrest, it is provocative to note that in one of the drawings, "a man is being beaten with a stick by one of the policemen, while his legs and arms are being held by three others; a fifth officer looks on, supervising the proceedings" (Franklin, 1970, p. 15).

During the period of conquest by the Roman Empire, under Emperor Augustus, the police were allowed to apply torture to anyone except citizens of Rome. Jesus Christ received the third-degree treatment; "he was brutally manhandled by those who arrested him, and beaten for not giving the right answers to the high priest" (Franklin, 1970, p. 17).

Deeley (1971) notes that the Inquisition, instituted by Pope Gregory IX in the 13th century and later led in Spain by the priest Torquemada, was "the forerunner of practices which are still used in many countries today" (p. 8). Even stool pigeons, placed in the suspect's cell to terrify him, were used back then. Under the implied blessing of the Roman Catholic church hierarchy, including Pope Innocent IV, excruciating tortures were carried out in search of heretics, primarily Jews. Not only did the methods of physical torture carry forward to the current century (and probably will into the next millennium), but so too we find vestiges of inquisitors' beliefs in the rightness of their acts—that the ends justify the means.

The Inquisition itself was not abolished until 1809. For more than 600 years its procedures reflected a realization that threat and psychological coercion could be effective. Eymeric, the Grand Inquisitor of Aragon, laid forth a guide for his brother priests that included five steps: "the threat of torture; taking the victim to the torture chamber, showing him the instruments (the Spaniards called them 'engines'), and explaining in detail how they worked; undressing and preparing the victim; placing him on a machine and tying him down; and finally, the torture itself" (Deeley, 1971, pp. 9-10). At each step, the inquisitor would remind the victim of the folly of remaining silent.

Perhaps surprisingly, given their heinousness, the tactics of the inquisitors were closely regulated. Lawyers were required to remain at the side of the heretic, and to note every word he said as he was tortured; they also recorded how long the torture lasted and what specific methods were used. The law was explicit that a man could not be tortured more than once unless new evidence came to light, but torturers could use whatever method they felt suitable to the case—deprivation of sleep, use of the rack, or of a water torture in which the victims feared they would suffocate (Deeley, 1971). When the victim was given a chance to confess, a lawyer would record his willingness or reluctance to talk. As Deeley observes, "in the name of legality, it was possible to carry out the most hideous practices" (1971, p. 12).

In another forerunner of more recent practices, the Holy Office stated that the confessions obtained as a result of such tortures were not valid unless they were later "voluntarily" ratified by the victim. As we have seen, in current police practice once a subject has orally confessed, the police draft a written statement of confession that the suspect is asked to sign under oath.

Joan of Arc, Savonarola, and Galileo were, of course, other famous victims of the Inquisition. Joan was subjected to prolonged and relentless questioning, accompanied by the threat of torture (Franklin, 1970). Savonarola was a priest in Florence who denounced the immoralities of the Papacy. After being tortured in 1498, he agreed to make any confession his inquisitors wished from him. Galileo was torn between his allegiance to the Church and his observations of the solar system as a scientist. Broken and ill at the age of 70, and having been shown the instruments of torture, he recanted his advocacy of the sun as the center of our planetary system.

The Salem witch trials, in Massachusetts in 1692, were an American manifestation of the use of torture to generate false confessions. Sleep deprivation, forced exercise such as standing for very long periods, and insertion of pins into the bodies of the young women were among the devices to get them to confess to their possession by Satan. Ann Foster, for example, confessed that the devil appeared to her in the shape of a bird on several occasions.

INTERROGATION IN OTHER COUNTRIES

Excessive amounts of interrogation are not limited to ancient times or contemporary America. The Communist purges instigated by Joseph Stalin in the Soviet Union were in some way like the extermination of witches in the Middle Ages (Deeley, 1971). The French used water torture, electric shock, and other tortures to gain information from dissidents during the civil war in Algeria in the 1950s (Vidal-Naquet, 1963). Gestapo tactics in Nazi Germany are so well known and infamous that the very term has become a shorthand expression for the use of coercion to create compliance. The security police in South Africa were responsible for the deaths of at least 200 black prisoners during a recent period (*Los Angeles Times,* 1992).

The British have long prided themselves as being the most humane of nations. As Deeley notes, "violence in the interview rooms of a British police station is a rare phenomenon" (1971, p. 40) but it does happen. In November of 1974 the Irish Republican Army blew up two pubs in Birmingham, England, killing 21 people and injuring more than 150 others. Within hours of the explosion six Irishmen (each of whom was living in England) were detained by the police. After 3 days of interrogation, four of them confessed. All six were put on trial, and each pleaded not guilty. The four said their confessions had been beaten out of them (Mullin, 1986). One, Paddy Hill, said that he had been kicked, punched in the side of his head, and kneed in the thigh. "We're going to get a statement out of you or kick you to death," he claimed he was told (Mullin, 1986, p. 100). These claims were rejected by the jury that found the Irishmen guilty; they were sentenced to life in prison. (On appeal, they were later released.)

AN ASSUMPTION OF GUILT

Prior to examining current interrogation practices in the United States, we need to answer the question: What determines whether or not a police officer decides a suspect is guilty, prior to an interrogation? Moston and Moston (1991) propose that the strength of the evidence against the suspect is likely to be a major influence on any presumption of guilt, but other factors—such as the age or race of the suspect and the nature of the crime—may also be influential.

But a second major influence is what might be called the demeanor or behavioral characteristics of the suspect, or the way in which the suspect behaves when in contact with the police (Moston & Moston, 1991). For example, when a suspect is initially questioned, are there cues in what is said or in the suspect's nonverbal behavior that lead the police to assume guilt?

Most suspects, truthfully or untruthfully, deny guilt upon initial questioning by the police. Are investigating officers able to detect deception? In general—and contrary to popular supposition—people are not very good at distinguishing between truth-telling and falsification; DePaulo, Stone, and Lassiter (1985) report about 45% to 60% accuracy, and Ekman and O'Sullivan go so far as to state: "Most liars can fool most people most of the time" (1989, p. 312).

Do law enforcement officers do better than laypersons in such a task? The evidence is mixed. DePaulo and Pfeifer (1986) found no difference between the accuracy levels of college students and federal law enforcement officers, when the task was identifying deception from an audiotape. But this would not have been an adequate test in several ways. More recently, Ekman and O'Sullivan (1991) report that even professionals—police investigators, judges, psychiatrists, and polygraphers for the FBI, CIA, and military—are prone to error. One of the problems in attaining accuracy is that the nonverbal cues that most assume to be associated with lying—avoiding eye contact, an increase in pitch of the voice, hesitation—may or may not be used more often by those who attempt to deceive.

INTERROGATION BY POLICE IN THE UNITED STATES

Popular Images of Interrogation

A bright light focused on the suspect's face . . . A rubber hose . . . A hot and crowded cell . . . The threat of further physical force and the promise of deprivation . . . Perhaps a team of "good cop and bad cop" . . . These and other images—maybe even ancient devices like the thumb-screw and the rack—contribute to our stereotype of the police interrogation. Even the word *interrogation* conjures up unnatural interactions; as Samuel Johnson, wrote, "Questioning is not a mode of conversation among gentlemen." The term *interrogation* is used generally to describe all questioning by police, regardless of whether it is conducted in custody or in the field, before or after arraignment. The term is preferred over "interviewing" because it implies a much more active role by the police detective (Macdonald & Michaud, 1987).

And it is conceded that such images were accurate in the past; the appellate cases described in Chapter 2 reflect the "third degree" tactics frequently used by police in the early years of this century. In limited localities and with selected suspects, they may still occur in America. Lawyers for Barry Lee Fairchild, a black man with an IQ score of 62, have claimed that he confessed to the murder of a white nurse only after Pulaski County (AR) sheriff's deputies "put telephone books on the top of his head and slammed downward repeatedly with blackjacks" (Lacayo, 1991, p. 27). Such actions cause excruciating pain but leave no marks as evidence of coercion. The sheriff of Pulaski County has denied Fairchild's claims (and Fairchild's conviction and death sentence are being appealed) but 11 other black men brought in for questioning about that time reported almost equally intimidating procedures; 3 said they had pistols placed in their mouths; officers pulled the trigger of the unloaded guns (Lacayo, 1991). A former sheriff's deputy even came forward and testified that he had seen the sheriff and other deputies abuse various suspects (Annin, 1990).

The Goals of Interrogators

Police and sheriff's department officers recognize that intimidating actions like those claimed by Barry Fairchild are illegal and often counterproductive. Some "confessions" created by such coercion do not withstand the scrutiny of a judge in a preliminary hearing. Most police believe that the *Miranda* warnings are a good idea; furthermore, police see themselves as members of a profession, which has an agreed-upon set of rules deriving partly from the laws, partly from common sense, and partly from tradition. These rules are systematized in several handbooks, developed for the use of police, which are described in Box 4.1. Also, police are briefed about new laws

BOX 4.1
Codifying Police Procedures

Four books provide police with instruction and guidelines regarding criminal investigations. Part of their coverage focuses on interrogations. They are:

1. *Fundamentals of Criminal Investigation,* by O'Hara and O'Hara (1980). Now in its fifth edition, this 900-page handbook devotes almost 100 pages to interrogations, confessions, and appropriate procedures by the police.

2. *The Gentle Art of Interviewing and Interrogation,* by Royal and Schutt (1976), is a more informal and readable manual that concentrates on interviewing and interrogation. Although we do not agree with all the opinions expressed by the authors, we recommend this book to anyone who wishes to learn what police are trained to do.

3. *Criminal Interrogation and Confessions,* by Inbau, Reid, and Buckley (1986). Now in its third edition, this book falls between the first two in length and style. It contains an excellent set of steps for questioning and eliciting confessions of suspects. Its authors facilitated the development and use of the polygraph, and the senior author is the John Henry Wigmore Professor of Law, Emeritus, at Northwestern University.

4. *The Confession: Interrogation and Criminal Profiles for Police Officers,* by Macdonald and Michaud (1987). A recent manual, written by a forensic psychiatrist and a police detective. Concentrates on interrogations leading to confessions. Contains a number of fascinating examples.

and court decisions that have impact on what is and is not acceptable procedure.

Contrary to the stereotype held by some, the handbooks state that the main goal for questioning suspects by the police is to gain information that furthers the investigation; "interrogation is not simply a means of inducing an admission of guilt," state O'Hara and O'Hara (1980, p. 111). Royal and Schutt (1976) agree: "The real objective of interrogation is the exploration and resolution of issues, not necessarily the gaining of a written or oral confession" (p. 25). Inbau, Reid, and Buckley (1986) advise: "Avoid creating the impression of an investigator seeking a confession or conviction. It is far better to fulfill the role of one who is merely seeking the truth" (p. 36). Certainly confessions, they say, are welcomed, but there are other goals. O'Hara and O'Hara (1980, pp. 110-111) list some of these as:

a. to obtain information concerning the innocence or guilt of the subject.
b. to obtain a confession to the crime from a guilty subject.
c. to induce the subject to make admissions.
d. to learn the facts and circumstances surrounding a crime.
e. to learn the identity of accomplices.
f. to learn of the existence and location of physical evidence such as documents and weapons.
g. to develop information which will lead to the fruits of the crime.
h. to develop additional leads for the investigation.
i. to discover the details of any other crimes in which the subject participated.

But these goals may be in conflict with each other; see Box 4.2.

A confession is desirable, but police realize that even if obtained, a confession may be refuted at trial. Police recognize that suspects confess for a variety of reasons, some of which may be unreliable. The greatest value of a confession may be that it leads to other, incriminating evidence. But even false statements are useful, because "the subject who lies is then committed to the psychological defense of a fantasy" (Royal & Schutt, 1976, p. 25).

Do police recognize that a confession may be false? They certainly try to distinguish these and verify each. Does the confession mesh with the facts of the case? Police especially view with skepticism the "conscience-stricken" confession. Box 4.3 summarizes a case in which the police detective in charge of a murder investigation was sensitive to the accuracy of a confession.

Interrogation Procedures

Part of the prevalent stereotype of police interrogation is the belief that the criminal is usually driven to confessing after having been trapped by the piercing brilliance of his or her interrogator (Deeley, 1971). "In reality," states a Scotland Yard detective,

BOX 4.2
Conflicting Goals in Interrogations

Irving and Hilgendorf (1980) observe that a police manual—like that of Inbau and Reid (1962)—sometimes is inconsistent about the primary goal of interrogation. Lloyd-Bostock (1989) summarizes their viewpoint:

Inbau and Reid are working with a dual notion of the causality of confessions and therefore are sometimes inconsistent in their advice. On the one hand they see confession as resulting from the suspect coming to believe that confession is the reasonable course of action but, on the other, they also sometimes view confession in terms of ["breaking"] the suspect. But overt threats, a build-up of stress and pressure, and displays of force tend to be counter-productive as a means of extracting a confession. There is a danger that the suspect will become over-aroused and this can produce a boomerang effect. When people (or animals) become very frightened, they respond by retreating or attacking. Similarly, an over-aroused suspect may withdraw co-operation in panic, or aggressively defy the interrogator. (p. 28)

Similarly, Inbau and Reid (1962) at one point advocate keeping the pressure on suspects who, close to the point of deciding to confess, begin to fidget and dither and show confusion—a procedure considered by psychologists (see Lloyd-Bostock, 1989) to be counter-productive. But at another point Inbau and Reid describe what Lloyd-Bostock calls a more promising approach to dealing with the suspect's conflict over making a decision; they suggest that the interrogator lead the subject away from the ultimate choice and thus take the pressure off, so that the suspect is not faced with making the critical choice until the optimum point in the questioning.

there is no sudden blinding shaft of light. You pick a villain [sic] up on something he said yesterday. . . . Usually it's a matter of wearing a person down. You may consider that a form of duress, but that's what it amounts to—wearing them down by persistence,

(text continued on page 71)

BOX 4.3
Did Harry Solberg Confess?

The Harry Solberg trial is an illustration of inconsistency. On a Tuesday afternoon in the spring of 1965 in Litchfield County, CT, a young housewife was brutally murdered in her own home. Her face and head were crushed, her jaw appeared to be broken, and her left temple was smashed in. There were stab marks at her throat, and knotted around her neck was an electrical cord pulled tight enough to strangle her. She had been hanged from the deck at the back of the house, and a trail of blood led from the kitchen and dining room through the house to the deck and below.

A piggy bank, containing about $20 in coins, was missing. The police later found a bloody steel-headed hammer in the woods behind the house, and a blood-stained 19-pound rock was discovered in the back yard.

Four days after the crime, the victim's husband received a letter saying, "I killed your wife. She worked with me at the bank. I told her if I couldn't have her no one would." The letter contained some details about the murder but nothing that hadn't been in the newspapers.

An anonymous confession by the murderer? Major Samuel Rome, chief of the detective division of the Connecticut State Police, was in charge of the investigation. On reading the letter, Rome immediately said, "This person is not the killer. He doesn't have the facts." Major Rome had, in fact, already identified the killer.

The victim's mother-in-law, Agnes Thompsen, lived with the victim and her husband and child. She was even there, in her upstairs apartment, the day of the murder. She claimed she had heard a couple of loud "thumps" during the afternoon and had looked out but had seen nothing. Ms. Thompsen has a history of mental illness; she had been hospitalized several times. In the evening after the murder was discovered, she was returned to the state hospital.

Reconstructing the crime, Major Rome concluded that (a) it was the work of a woman, (b) it was the act of an insane person, and (c) it was done by someone who had time, who was not in a hurry to get away. The coroner issued a tentative finding that Agnes Thompsen was "criminally suspect," and Major Rome announced that in his mind the case was solved. Four months after the murder, the coroner found there "was reasonable cause to believe that Agnes Thompsen was criminally responsible." A warrant was issued against Valley Hospital—a technicality to permit her arrest if the hospital ever chose to release her. Nobody, however, suggested that. Major Rome closed the case.

But in March 1966—9 months after the murder—it was announced that the police had arrested one Harry Solberg and charged him with the murder. At the time of the crime, Harry was still a high school student. He had progressed slowly through school, taking 5 years to complete the usual 3 years of high school.

Harry had been picked up by the police on Sunday morning, March 13, 1966, and taken to the Canaan Barracks for questioning and then, in the afternoon, to the Hartford headquarters for a lie detector test. He was questioned almost continuously from 9:30 a.m. until that evening. During the afternoon he apparently admitted to writing the letter. (Later he said he had done it to direct suspicion away from himself, as he had a black 1959 Ford similar to the one spotted in the neighborhood the afternoon of the murder. In his simple-minded way, Harry thought the letter would remove suspicion from him.)

Harry was told that the results of the lie detector test were not satisfactory, and he was asked to take another on Monday. He readily agreed to. On Sunday evening, about 9:00 p.m., he went home with his parents, promising to return Monday after work. Shortly after he completed a second polygraph test on that day, he was booked for the murder of Dorothy Thompsen. Apparently Harry Solberg had confessed to the crime.

He later told his attorney that he had stopped at the Thompsen house the afternoon of the murder to get some information about a paper he was required to write for his high school economics class. The front door was halfway open and he could hear the baby crying. As he walked into the Thompsen house, he could see blood all over everything. He followed the trail of blood out to the deck and the backyard. "And that's all I remember," he told his attorney. He had got in his car and driven aimlessly around the countryside.

But it is true that Harry had given the police a sort of confession. He had told the police he couldn't remember much else, except climbing the ladder down from the deck. Regarding the bloody hammer found in the woods, all he said he remembered was throwing it. Intensively asked about the serving fork, another murder weapon, he had said to the police "I must have used it on her, but that's all I can remember about it too." Later during the police interrogation, Harry reportedly said, "I guess I stabbed her and beat her."

The police considered that to be enough for a confession. In addition, handwriting experts concluded that Harry had written the letter, and the missing piggy bank was found one-half mile from his house.

But the reaction of Major Rome (who was now off the case) was quite different:

> That's not a confession! It tells you nothing! A statement isn't a confession until it's corroborated. When you get a confession you take the person right out to the scene of the crime and make him re-enact it there exactly the way it happened. You make him prove it. Solberg doesn't tell them anything. He can't. He doesn't know. He says he must have hit her with a hammer. . . . Police interrogation is an art. You have to let the person tell you. You purposely try to mislead him, and if you can't, then you know. You ask questions that will tell you: *Could* he have seen this? *Could* he have caused this? . . . We've thrown out dozens of false confessions.

But the police persisted, and the district attorney offered Harry Solberg a plea bargain: plead guilty to manslaughter and receive a lesser prison sentence. His attorney told Harry, "If you're guilty you'd better take it." Harry responded, "All right, maybe we'd better take it." But the attorney said, "First, you'll have to tell me how you did it, or the judge won't accept it." Harry then reported, "I can't remember." So, he, his father, and his attorney decided he'd better stand trial.

In Harry Solberg's trial, the judge had no difficulty in concluding the confession was voluntary and hence admissible in evidence. He ruled that "the procedures followed by the state police were entirely proper and in keeping with the rights of the individual" (Savage, 1970, p. 179). The trial began on schedule, and the police report of the interrogation was included as part of the evidence against Solberg. But once the jury began to deliberate, it apparently struggled over the legitimacy of the confession, because after several days of deliberation, the foreperson reported the jury was hung. (Later rumors had it that the vote was 10-2, but the direction was unclear. The judge believed it was in favor of guilt, but Solberg's attorney heard that it was 10-2 for acquittal.) The judge ruled a mistrial, and a second trial was scheduled for 3 months later.

So, in January 1967, a year and a half after the crime, a second trial for Harry Solberg was begun—with a different judge and in a different city. But it ended quickly; the new judge concluded that

> the interrogation procedures used by the police had violated the defendant's *Miranda* rights and ruled that the confession could not be introduced as evidence. No longer having the strong evidence he needed to support a conviction for murder, the district attorney filed a substitute indictment: for "malicious threatening under the blackmail statute," referring to Harry's sending the letter. Harry Solberg pleaded guilty to this charge and was sentenced to prison for 1 to 10 years.
>
> Source: Adapted from Savage, 1970.

like water dripping on a stone. Not brilliance. (quoted by Deeley, 1971, p. 139)

Prior planning is one facilitator of a successful crime investigation. Police detectives first need to ask themselves if the questioning of a suspect is potentially the most valuable means of getting the desired information under the existing circumstances (Royal & Schutt, 1976). If it is decided to question suspects, prior to this the police officer should read all the investigation reports and statements already taken, visit the scene of the crime, check out suspects' alibis, examine any previous criminal records of suspects, and make inquiries of other people who may have relevant information (Macdonald & Michaud, 1987; Royal & Schutt, 1976). One detective has commented:

The more you know about the man you are going to interrogate the better position you are in to know his weak points. I had a case where I could have talked till hell froze over and this guy wouldn't have confessed. But another policeman had supplied me with a tiny scrap of information beforehand which opened him up. (quoted by Deeley, 1971, p. 142)

It is important to view the interrogation as a dialogue between two persons, each with his or her goals for the outcome of the social interaction (Moston, Stephenson, & Williamson, 1991). As indicated, the police officer seeks useful information at the very least, if not a confession. The suspect seeks release, or perhaps, a promise of lenient treatment if a confession is offered. Each comment by each participant has a direct effect on the next comment by the other. A suspect's responses will be assessed through an implicit cost-benefit analysis, specifically a calculation of the relative advantages of different responses; what response—albeit inconsistent from his or her earlier responses—is now likely to move the person toward his or her goal?

The Physical Setting

To begin with, police manuals (most notably Inbau et al.'s *Criminal Interrogation and Confessions,* 1986) urge officials to employ a specifically constructed room that is psychologically removed from the sights and sounds of the police station, and to maintain rigid control over the ecology of that interrogation room. The novelty of this facility serves the function of giving the suspect "the illusion that the environment itself is withdrawing further and further away" (Aubry & Caputo, 1965, p. 38). Inbau et al. (1986) go so far as to conclude that privacy—being alone with the suspect—is "the principal psychological factor contributing to a successful interrogation" (p. 24).

To further minimize sensory stimulation and remove all extraneous sources of distraction, social support, and relief from tension, the manuals recommend that the interrogation be done in a small room that is acoustically soundproofed and bare, without furniture or ornaments—only two chairs and perhaps a desk (see, for example, Macdonald & Michaud, 1987, p. 15). Also critical, of course, is that the accused be denied communicative access to friends and family. Finally, the interrogator is advised to sit as close as possible to the subject, in armless, straight-backed chairs, and at equal eye level. Invading the suspect's personal space, it is said, will increase his or her level of anxiety from which the only means of escape is confession, as well as maintaining the suspect's attention and establishing an attitude of understanding.

In a similar vein, the police manual by Royal and Schutt advises:

Almost without exception, subjects and unfriendly witnesses should be removed from familiar surroundings. Most persons feel more secure and, accordingly, more contented in their homes or offices. In addition, they feel a necessity to maintain personal integrity before family, friends, and neighbors. Removing a person from familiar locations eliminates those barriers and initiates the process of getting him into a submissive or "yes" mood. It also permits taking him to a location and atmosphere that is conducive to cooperation and truthfulness. (1976, pp. 56-57)

The one exception to this rule can occur immediately after a crime has been committed, if a suspect indicates that he or she is willing to talk (Macdonald & Michaud, 1987).

Interestingly, Royal and Schutt advise against the use of primitive conditions:

A room should be private and the furniture comfortable. There should be no glaring lights or signs of restraint. . . . Use of bare, gray-walled interrogation room is tantamount to a modern "star chamber." . . . A location that has a cheerful, "You have nothing to fear quality" about it can do much to break down pre-interview defensiveness. (1976, p. 57)

Both O'Hara and O'Hara (1980) and Inbau et al. (1986) instruct police interrogators to dress in regular clothes—and conservative ones, at that: "Civilian dress is more likely to inspire confidence and friendship in a criminal than a uniform. The accoutrements of the police profession should be removed from view. The sight of a protruding gun or billy may arouse enmity or a defensive attitude on the part of the criminal" (p. 114).

In keeping with the above constraints, police interviewers are advised to avoid letting the suspect establish the ground rules. The most common procedure is the "stipulation"; the subject will attempt to set down a set of ground rules that he wants followed. He may say, "I will answer any questions about 'X' or 'Y' or 'Z' but not others" (Royal & Schutt, 1976, p. 67). Female suspects may employ seductive behavior or crying to try to control the situation. In response, the interviewer needs to display firmness and authority, without reflecting arrogance. Macdonald and Michaud (1987) suggest that the interrogator convey to the suspect some piece of information about him, such as his full name and birth date. Emphasis in the manuals, such as the one by Inbau et al., on establishing authority are consistent with the findings of psychological research. As Lloyd-Bostock (1989) observes, the relationship between an individual and someone in authority potentially can generate quite dramatic psychological effects. Stanley Milgram's (1974) well-known series of studies on obedience showed the appalling degree to which ordinary people would obey the instructions of an experimenter who had established a position of authority. Subjects in his studies were willing to follow instructions to administer painful and dangerous electric shocks to other subjects. Lloyd-Bostock (1989) concludes that suspects being interrogated can become, like Milgram's subjects, just as acquiescent to the demands of an interrogator who has carefully established control over the situation.

Inbau et al. advise interrogators to confront suspects early in the session, and tell them they are involved in a crime. They should anticipate denials by suspects, but stop a deceptive suspect's denial even before it is completed. They alert interrogators to note how suspects react to this admonition; Inbau et al. believe innocent suspects become stronger in reaffirming their denials, whereas deceptive subjects stop claiming alibis or excuses.

The Content of Interrogations

We have noted that the handbooks for police emphasize the need to be professional in conducting investigations and interrogations. Beyond the previously described reasons for restraint, too much pressure may put the accused in such an emotional state that his or her capacity for rational judgment is impaired. Manuals suggest opening with a positive statement: "We're investigating an armed robbery and we think you can help us" (Macdonald & Michaud,

1987, p. 19). But the question remains: What other kinds of devices do police use in questioning suspects? What are the limits? Recent analyses of police work are instructive. Leo concludes that "manipulation and deception have replaced force and direct coercion as the strategic underpinnings of information-gathering techniques that police now employ during criminal investigation" (1992, p. 35). Gary Marx even observes: "There is an interesting irony at work here: restrict police use of coercion, and the use of deception increases" (1988, p. 47).

Methods of Interrogation

Despite the persistence of controversy surrounding police methods of criminal investigation, surprisingly little exists in the way of empirical documentation of interrogation practices.

Back in 1931, the U.S. National Commission on Law Observance and Enforcement published a report of its findings and confirmed the worst fears about police abuse, noting that the use of severe third-degree tactics to extract confessions was at that time "widespread" (p. 153). As examples, the Commission cited as commonplace the use of physical violence, methods of intimidation adjusted to the age and mentality of the accused, refusal to give access to counsel, fraudulent promises that could not be fulfilled, and prolonged illegal detention. In an effort to characterize the interrogation process as it might have changed since that time, the Supreme Court in its *Miranda v. Arizona* (1966) decision—lacking direct observational or interview data—turned for evidence of what transpires to actual reported cases involving coerced confessions and to a review of the most popular manuals then available for advising law enforcement officials about successful tactics for eliciting confessions (see Aubry & Caputo, 1965; Inbau & Reid, 1962; O'Hara & O'Hara, 1956). Essentially, the Court concluded from its inquiry that "the modern practice of in-custody interrogation is (now) psychologically rather than physically oriented" (*Miranda v. Arizona*, p. 448), but that the degree of coerciveness inherent in the situation had not diminished. Writing in 1966, the Court's majority opinion, written by Chief Justice Earl Warren, noted "the use of physical brutality and violence is not, unfortunately, relegated to the past" (p. 446). Have matters changed in the three subsequent decades?

Manipulative Tactics. Inbau and Reid (1962) described in considerable detail 16 overlapping strategies with which confessions could be elicited from initially recalcitrant suspects. From them, three major themes emerge. The first is to reconceptualize for the suspect the attributional implications of his or her crime by minimizing its seriousness (e.g., "It's not all that unusual" or "I've seen thousands of others in the same situation") or by providing a face-saving external attribution of blame ("on the spur of the moment you did this"). The interrogator might, for example, suggest to the suspect that there were extenuating circumstances in his or her particular case, providing such excusing conditions as self-defense, passion, or simple negligence. Or the blame might be shifted onto a specific person such as the victim or an accomplice. Often the suspect is asked if the act was victim precipitated. Inbau and Reid (1962) offered the following example of how such attributional manipulation has been used successfully as bait: A middle-aged man, accused of having taken indecent liberties with a 10-year-old girl, was told that "this girl is well developed for her age. She probably learned a lot about sex from boys . . . she may have deliberately tried to excite you to see what you would do." In another documented instance, Wald, Ayres, Hess, Schantz, and Whitebread (1967) observed a detective tell a breaking-and-entering suspect that "the guy should never have left all that liquor in the window to tempt honest guys like you and me" (p. 1544).

From an entirely different angle, an alternative strategy is to frighten the suspect into confessing. One way to accomplish this is by exaggerating the seriousness of the offense and magnitude of the charges. In theft or embezzlement cases, for example, the reported loss—and hence the consequences of a convicted defendant—could be increased. Another variation of the scare tactic is for the interrogator to presume to have a firm belief about the suspect's culpability based in independent, "factual" evidence. Police manuals are replete with specific suggestions about how to use what is referred to as the "knowledge-bluff" trick. The interrogator could thus pretend to have strong circumstantial evidence (e.g., the suspect's fingerprints at the scene of the crime), have a policeman pose as an eyewitness and identify the suspect in a rigged line-up, or even—through elaborate staging devices—try to persuade the suspect that he or she has already been implicated by an accomplice or co-suspect. Another interesting technique, along similar lines, is to focus the suspect in on his or her apparent psychophysiological and nonverbal indicators of a guilty conscience such as dryness of the mouth, sweating, fidgety bodily movements, or downcast eyes.

"Baiting questions" are sometimes employed if this approach is chosen. These are not accusatory in nature but still convey to suspects that some evidence exists linking them to the crime. For example, the detective may ask: "Jim, is there any reason you can think of why one of Mary's neighbors would say that your car was seen parked in front of her home that night?" Without waiting for an answer, the interrogator would then say: "Now, I'm not accusing you of anything; maybe you just stopped by to see if Mary was at home" (Inbau et al., 1986, p. 69). Sometimes baiting questions carry the strong implication that the answer is already known to the police, when in fact it is not. Their goal remains to get the suspect tacitly to acknowledge involvement in the crime.

Similar in its anticipated effect is to tell a suspect that he or she has failed a polygraph test. As a deceptive practice, this action is justified by police because it may cause a guilty suspect to confess. In fact, some polygraph examiners will readily acknowledge that a basic purpose for giving the test is to encourage law breakers to admit their crimes. Examiners will use tricks to intimidate a suspect, to convince the subject that the machine is infallible.

The third general type of approach is based on the development of a personal rapport with the suspect. Referring to this as the emotional appeal, police manuals advise the interrogator to show sympathy, understanding, and respect through flattery and gestures such as the offer of a drink. Establishing eye contact is important. Having established a friendly relationship, the interrogator might then try to persuade the suspect that confessing is in his or her own best interests. In a more elaborate version of this strategy, two detectives enact a "Mutt and Jeff" (or "good-cop, bad-cop") routine in which one comes across as hostile and relentless, while the other gains the suspect's confidence by being protective and supportive. This technique is apparently quite common, and was used in a case described by Zimbardo (1967). In addition to these various specific strategies, the literature reviewed by the Supreme Court in *Miranda* contained several universally applicable rules of thumb, the most important of which is "an oppressive atmosphere of dogged persistence." Not surprisingly, the Court concluded from its findings that the interrogation practices were inherently coercive. As we note in Chapter 3 and in a later section of this chapter, the viewpoint of the Supreme Court has changed from this adamant position.

Direct Observational Data. Are the admittedly indirect and poorly sampled data culled by the Supreme Court an accurate depiction of the interrogation process or do they portray only the most atypical and extreme forms of coercion? In an empirical study, Wald et al. (1967) observed 127 interrogations over the course of 11 weeks in the New Haven, CT, Police Department. In addition to recording the frequency with which various tactics were used in these sessions, the investigators interviewed the police officers and attorneys involved as well as some ex-suspects.

Overall, this research revealed that one or more of the tactics recommended by Inbau and Reid (1962) were employed in 65% of the interrogations observed, and that the detectives used an average of two tactics per suspect. The most common approach was to overwhelm the suspect with damaging evidence, to assert a firm belief in his guilt, and then to suggest that it would be easier for all concerned if the suspect admitted to his role in the crime. This latter plea was often accompanied by a show of sympathy and concern for the suspect's welfare. Most of the other methods cited in the manuals were also used with varying frequency, including the Mutt-and-Jeff routine, playing off co-suspects, minimizing the seriousness of the offense, shifting the blame for the crime to external factors, and alerting the suspect to signs of nervousness that reveal a guilty conscience. The investigators reported that no undue physical force was used by the detectives, but they did observe the frequent use of promises (e.g., offers of lowered bail, reduced charges, and judicial leniency) and vague threats about harsher treatment. In three instances, suspects were told that the police would make trouble for their families and friends if they refused to cooperate.

Wald et al. (1967) concluded from their observations that the New Haven detectives employed most of the persuasive techniques listed by Inbau and Reid, thus justifying, to some extent, the Court's fears. When these tactics were combined with a generally hostile demeanor and lengthy interrogation, they often appeared to be successful. Moreover, it is perhaps reasonable to speculate that because the mere presence of observers at the sessions could have inhibited the use of stronger forms of pressure, these results might even underestimate the coercion employed during interrogation.

In the United Kingdom, Barrie Irving and Linden Hilgendorf (1980) carried out a similar study, by observing interrogations carried out by the CID at Brighton. They classified police interviewing techniques on the basis of how well they altered the suspect's view of the consequences of confessing or not confessing. These consequences are either utilitarian ones, social consequences, or effects on the suspect's self-esteem.

For example, if the interrogators chose to downgrade the seriousness of the crime, it could affect the utilitarian consequences for the suspect who thus confessed. Irving (1980) observed interrogators telling suspects that if they made a clean breast of things it would increase the likelihood of their receiving lenient treatment in court. (In the United Kingdom, the Police and Criminal Evidence Act of 1984 changed the rules of what were acceptable interrogation procedures.)

Other police interrogators skillfully developed a relationship with suspects, so that the interrogator's own approval had social consequences for the suspect. The police officer might express sympathy, understanding, or empathy with the suspect's actions, thus downplaying the negative social consequences that might follow conviction (Lloyd-Bostock, 1989).

Or, the interrogator may attempt to alter the way a suspect views himself, by emphasizing the suspect's good sense or likeable nature, or pointing out how much better it would feel to get things off one's chest, thus attempting to have effects on the suspect's self-esteem (Irving & Hilgendorf, 1980).

The Limits of Acceptability. Among the manipulative psychological techniques described above, we have assumed that most people would probably consider as the most unpalatable the following (in ascending order): promises, threats, and lies. State and federal appellate courts have, since *Miranda,* ruled on each of these procedures, but a general guideline for each is to ask: "Is the action something that is likely to cause the subject to make a false confession?" If it is, it should not be employed.

1. Promises. As a general rule, for a promise to invalidate a confession, it must have reference to the subject's escape from punishment or the mitigation of his or her punishment. A promise to the suspect that if he confesses he will be released from custody, that he will not be prosecuted, that he will be granted a pardon, or that he will receive a lighter sentence than the law prescribes will invalidate a confession (Inbau et al., 1986). Such an invalidation holds even if the interrogator merely states that he will do whatever he can do to induce the proper authorities to grant such immunity or reduction of a sentence. Likewise, a kind of plea bargain—telling the subject who is accused of a number of crimes that if he confesses to one, he will not be prosecuted for the others—nullifies the confession.

But promises to offer the subject greater comfort or gratification of other personal desires are not grounds to throw out the confession, nor are promises to keep the subject's confession a secret (Inbau et al., 1986).

2. Threats. Psychological coercion is of concern to the courts. Moral restraint by means of threat can destroy the voluntariness of a confession. "Obliquely suggesting the prospect of harm to the suspect, his relatives, or his property can be interpreted as psychological abuse even though these suggestions do not assume the form of explicit threats" (O'Hara & O'Hara, 1980, pp. 142-143). The question is: Does the subject reasonably think he or she is in sufficient danger? Examples include: telling a suspect he will be turned over to a mob unless he confesses, or threatening to "throw the book at him" if he doesn't confess.

In contrast, the courts have permitted interrogators to use the following techniques:

1. to tell the suspect that, after all, the police are going to discover the truth anyway.
2. to inform the subject that he may tell whatever he wishes and run the risk of imprisonment.
3. to display impatience with the subject's story.
4. to give the underlying impression that the interrogator considers the subject guilty. (O'Hara & O'Hara, 1980, p. 143)

3. Trickery and Deception. Deceit is generally repugnant in our society. Police manuals strongly differ about its acceptability in interrogations. On the one hand, Macdonald and Michaud advise police:

> Do not make any false statements. Do not tell him his finger-prints were found at the scene if they were not found at the scene. Do not tell him he was identified by an eyewitness if he was not identified by an eyewitness. If he catches you in a false statement, he will no longer trust you, he will assume that you do not have sufficient evidence to prove his guilt, and his self-confidence will go up. (1978, p. 23)

But some police investigators (see, e.g., Inbau et al., 1986) believe that without some elements of trickery, leading the suspect to believe that the police have some tangible or specific evidence of guilt, many interrogations would be totally ineffective.

As Inbau et al. (1986) observe: "Although recent Supreme Court opinions have contained derogatory statements about 'trickery' and 'deceit' as interrogation devices, no case has prohibited their usage" (p. 320). What if deceit is used to generate a confession? Once more, the working rule in most state courts is the following: Trickery and deception may be used if they are not of such a nature as to be likely to lead the subject into a false confession (O'Hara & O'Hara, 1980). Among the deceptions considered permissible by the state courts are informing the subject that his accomplice has confessed and pretending that cogent evidence such as his fingerprints or additional witnesses exist. The use of such ruses has not been prohibited by the U.S. Supreme Court.

The case of *State v. Jackson* (1983) in North Carolina is illustrative. James Jackson, who was suspected of murder, was falsely told by the police that blood stains from the victim were on his pants, that his shoes matched footprints found at the crime scene, and that he was spotted by an eyewitness. He also reassured that if he "told the truth" (i.e., if he confessed), the judge would view him as cooperative. Jackson then confessed, telling what appeared to be an implausible story. After being charged with murder, he retracted the confession, claiming that he had been coerced. He appealed his murder conviction but the North Carolina Supreme Court ruled that his confession was voluntary, and that it should not be invalidated by the use of trickery. Jackson, they noted, had not been physically restrained, promised a light sentence, or directly threatened.

Given that the courts have given the green light to the use of such procedures by the police, what is their effect upon jurors? (Chapter 6 treats jurors' general reactions to coerced confessions but it is also appropriate at this point to look at their reactions to these specific procedures.)

If we reconsider the manipulative tactics described earlier, they can be classified into two differing types. Kassin and McNall (1991) label one type as *maximization,* a "hard sell" technique in which the interrogator tries to scare and intimidate the suspect into confessing. For example, he might make false claims about evidence (the "presence" of an eyewitness, or a "failed" lie-detector test) and he might exaggerate the seriousness of the offense and the magnitude of the charges. The second approach, called *minimization,* uses a "soft sell" technique in which the police interrogator may try to lull the suspect into a false sense of security by offering sympathy, tolerance, face-saving excuses, or even moral justification. Or he may play down the seriousness of the charges, blame an accomplice or even the victim, or cite extenuating circumstances.

What effect might these tactics have on the unwary suspect? Although there is no way to know for sure, it is possible that minimization implies an offer of leniency, whereas maximization implies a threat of punishment. To test this hypothesis, Kassin and McNall (1991) had subjects read transcripts of interrogations in which the detective made an explicit promise or an explicit threat, or used minimization, maximization, or none of the above. They then assessed sentencing expectations for the suspect who confesses, and for the one who denies the charges but is later found guilty. The results: (a) Subjects expected the suspect to receive a more severe sentence if found guilty than if he or she confessed, (b) maximization aroused expectations for the harshest sentence, and (c) minimization aroused expectations for leniency. In other words, maximization— where the interrogator tries to frighten the suspect by exaggerating the evidence and the charges—communicates an implicit threat of punishment. And minimization—where the interrogator lulls the suspect into a false sense of security by mitigating the crime, making excuses, or blaming the victim—communicates an implicit offer of leniency. Yet while the courts routinely exclude confessions elicited by explicit threats and promises, they admit those produced by these other tactics.

F I V E

Why People Confess

Psychological Perspectives

In a review that has not received the attention it deserves, Bedau and Radelet (1987) identified 350 examples in the United States alone of miscarriages of justice; in each of these an innocent person or persons were convicted of murder. For 49 of these cases, the primary reason for the conviction was a false confession generated by a coercive questioning.

The Earl of Birkenhead, in his book *More Famous Trials* (1938), describes one of the earliest documented cases of a confession proved to be false. The case, back in 1660, involved the confession of John Perry to the alleged murder of William Harrison. As a result, John Perry, his mother, and his brother were all convicted of murder on the basis of Perry's confession alone, even though it was retracted at the trial. No other evidence existed that Harrison had been murdered or that the Perrys were involved, but circumstantial evidence linked John Perry to Harrison's disappearance. During an extensive questioning John Perry made a statement to the Justice of the Peace implicating his mother, his brother, and himself in the alleged murder. All three were executed, but 2 years later the supposed murder victim reappeared very much alive (Gudjonsson & MacKeith, 1990).

How often does this happen? We do not know, but Lloyd-Bostock (1989) reports that in the United Kingdom, false confessions ranked second only to mistaken identifications as a cause of wrongful conviction among cases referred to the Court of Appeal. To measure the actual validity of confession evidence, we would need to assess the combined frequency with which truly guilty suspects confess and truly innocent suspects do not. This goal is, of course, impossible to attain. But we can at least delineate the possibilities. Two types of erroneous outcome are possible—those probably common instances in which guilty suspects failed to confess ("misses" in signal detection terms) and the probably rarer occasions when suspects who are actually innocent do confess ("false alarms" in signal detection terms). Because our accusatorial system of justice protects the individual's right to refuse self-incrimination, the first type of error does not provide a source of concern for those who subscribe to a belief that it is the prosecution's task to prove guilt beyond a reasonable doubt.

The second category of error, however, does pose a serious problem for the courts. In assessing the trustworthiness of confession evidence, the questions we ask in this chapter are: What is the risk of false confessions, and why do false confessions occur? A later section of the chapter considers psychological theorizing and research on the therapeutic nature of confession.

TYPES OF FALSE CONFESSIONS

It is impossible to determine or even estimate the frequency with which people confess to crimes that they did not actually commit. Is there a reasonable risk of false confessions? Although the layperson might find it difficult to believe, enough instances have been documented to suggest that concern over such a risk is justified (Barthel, 1976; Borchard, 1932; Foster, 1969; Münsterberg, 1908; Note, 1953; Reik, 1959; Sutherland, 1965; Wigmore, 1937; Zimbardo, 1967).

Why do such false confessions occur? Brandon and Davies (1972) examined cases in which defendants had been convicted mostly on the basis of their own confession, and subsequently the conviction had been overturned or the defendant pardoned. They concluded that many of these defendants possessed similar types of qualities; these clustered in three categories: low intelligence and/or illiteracy, youthful age, and a mental disturbance such as depression.

Voluntary False Confessions

A perusal of the anecdotal literature led Kassin and Wrightsman (1985) to distinguish among three psychologically distinct types of false confessions: (a) voluntary, (b) coerced-compliant, and (c) coerced-internalized. *Voluntary false confessions,* those purposefully offered in the absence of elicitation, are on the face of it the most enigmatic of the three types. Why, for example, did more than 200 people confess to the famous Lindbergh baby kidnapping? Apparently, a "morbid desire for notoriety" could account for many of these as well as other examples in which numbers of false confessions are received for widely publicized crimes (see Note, 1953, p. 382). Other suggested motives for voluntary false confessions include the unconscious need to expiate guilt over previous transgressions via self-punishment, the hope for a recommendation of leniency, and a desire to aid and protect the real criminal (Gudjonsson & MacKeith, 1988). Then, of course, innumerable examples exist in which false confessions are offered by individuals subsequently diagnosed as mentally ill and unable to distinguish between fantasy and reality (see Guttmacher & Weihofen, 1952). Irving's (1980) study of Brighton (United Kingdom) interrogations concluded that nearly half the subjects interviewed could be described as being in an abnormal state.

The risk of voluntary false confessions was illustrated in a murder case recently tried in the state of Wisconsin. The district attorney showed the jury a videotape of the defendant's confession. In that same case, however, the defense lawyer noted that the police had also received confessions from three other individuals unrelated to the defendant. One of these was a young woman who voluntarily stepped forward to implicate herself and a group of motorcyclists. The problem? In the following poignant letter, written to the police, this woman later admitted that she had fabricated the initial story in order to satisfy her pathological need for attention and approval:

Dear Sergeant:

You probably aren't going to understand everything that I will be telling you in this letter, because I really have a hard time explaining what's going on with me, but for myself, I have to try. All of my life I was seeking attention. I wanted to hear from people that they cared and that I was loved. I tried being a jock and be a great athlete to get attention and it worked for a while, but then there was always someone better than me and I became very insecure. I wasn't getting the love and attention that I was looking for.

I soon began doing anything for attention, even if it was negative attention. I became what is commonly called a slut, I began using drugs and alcohol, I stole, I lied, I used people and all of these negative things I did, I got attention and people told me they loved me and they cared about me. I even had suicide attempts because I wanted help.

I became a person who would do anything just to be accepted. I came to really realize that today. Because, up until now, that's what I've been doing and it's only hurting myself. . . . It was a cycle. And I am having a hard time breaking that pattern . . . I went to see a "shrink" and he won't make me a client because I can't pay him. At that point, I wanted to commit suicide.

One of the risks I have to do is to tell you the things in this letter. I know that I could have big trouble for lying to the police dept. about the bikers and stuff and I guess I am asking you for your understanding and forgiveness. I don't know who murdered M. C. and I honestly don't think it was these bikers. I got so deep into the lie and it seemed like I couldn't get out. I couldn't admit to the people that I lied to that I liked because they would stop caring. Look who all of that attention hurt! I hurt myself. I want it to stop. When lying becomes a part of your life, you become good at it. And I am good at it. But I want to quit. . . . Please believe me that I have only told you the truth in this letter . . . I want to be free of these lies and the only way I can do it is if I open up and be honest.

I would appreciate it if you would keep this between me and you. I need to know that I can trust people. If you could read this as a person and not a cop I think you will find some understanding

of what I'm trying to say to you and understand that I want help
and am looking for help.
  I really am sorry for what I have done to you and I hope that
you can forgive me. I want you to like me, Sergeant.
  Thanks for listening,
                                 L. V.

Coerced-Compliant Confessions

  In contrast to those occasions when individuals voluntarily initiate
false confessions are those in which suspects confess through the
coerciveness of the interrogation process. Within this category of
coerced false confessions, a further distinction should be drawn.
Psychologists have long recognized the importance of two concep-
tually different responses to social control attempts: compliance and
internalization (Kelman, 1958). Compliance is an overt, public acquiescence to a social influence attempt in order to achieve some
immediate instrumental gain, whereas internalization is a personal
acceptance of the values or beliefs espoused in that attempt.
  Two well-known social-psychological demonstrations reflect compliance: Asch (1958) found that some people will go along with the
majority in their estimates of line lengths, even when they knew their
public report was false, and Milgram (1974) discovered that some of
his subjects would obediently administer shocks to another person
who was in great pain.
  Two meaningful differences between the two closely related processes of compliance and internalization have been observed. First,
whereas compliance is reflected in subsequent behavior only if it
continues to have instrumental value, internalized behaviors persist
over time and across a variety of situations. Second, it appears that
although immediate compliance is most effectively elicited through
powerful and highly salient techniques of social control, internalization
is best achieved through more subtle, less coercive methods (see Lepper,
1983, for a self-perception theory explanation of this phenomenon).
  In view of the foregoing distinction, it is clear that some false
confessions may be viewed as *coerced-compliant,* wherein the sus-

pect publicly professes guilt in response to extreme methods of interrogation, despite knowing privately that he or she is truly innocent (see Box 5.1 for an example).

Reflecting the instrumental component of such conduct, Wigmore (1970) noted that one of the main reasons for distrusting confession evidence arises "when a person is placed in such a situation that an untrue confession of guilt has become the more desirable of two alternatives between which the person was obliged to choose" (p. 344). Historically, many of the false confessions extracted through torture, threats, and promises were probably of this type. And, reflecting the nonpermanent character of "mere" compliance, such confessions are typically withdrawn and hence challenged at the pretrial voluntariness hearing. Perhaps the best known example is one discussed in Chapter 2, *Brown v. Mississippi* (1936), in which the defendant confessed after having been whipped with steel-studded belts, and then maintained—upon appeal—that he made false selfincriminating statements in order to escape and avoid the painful beatings.

Relevant to the forced-compliant category are most of the cases of "brainwashing" of American prisoners of war. Almost 40 years ago, during the Korean War, Americans learned from reports by the North Koreans that a number of captured American military men had confessed to a number of treasonable acts and expressions of disloyalty to the United States. The news created a national scandal (see Kinkead, 1959); commentators asked if American young men were "lacking in the moral character necessary to take a difficult and possibly dangerous stand on the basis of their principles" (Fleming & Scott, 1991, p. 129). It even led to a U.S. military Code of Conduct, which instructed captured military personnel to give only their name, rank, serial number, and birth date to their captors.

Despite this, similar confessions were made by some of the American POWs in the Vietnam War, and during the first week of the Persian Gulf War, viewers saw on their television screens the grim and swollen faces of seven captured American airmen; "each of the pilots identified himself and delivered a short speech deploring their government's involvement in Operation Desert Storm" (Fleming & Scott, 1991, p. 127).

BOX 5.1
An Example of a Coerced-Compliant Confession

In 1987 two frail and elderly women in England were found battered to death in their home. Apparently they had been sexually assaulted, and their savings were missing.

Several days later a 17-year-old neighboring boy was arrested and questioned extensively, simply because after the murders he had been spending more money than usual. No physical evidence linked him to the murders. He was denied access to a lawyer.

The interrogation began 3½ hours after his arrest and lasted nearly 14 hours, with various breaks during this period. Five different officers took turns questioning him. They claimed to have witnesses who had seen him near the victims' house about the time of the murder. The boy repeatedly denied this, but in response to many leading and accusatory questions, he began to show clear signs of distress, including sobbing, shaking, and crying. "He gradually began to give in to the police officer's questioning, at first admitting he had been out at the material time and then that he had been near the victim's house" (Gudjonsson & MacKeith, 1990, p. 331). Later on he gave a detailed self-incriminating admission about the two murders, the sexual assaults, and the theft. However, the next day, during further questioning, he retracted his confession, explaining that he had falsely confessed previously because of persistent and repeated pressure from the different police officers interviewing him (Gudjonsson & MacKeith, 1990).

During the year that he was kept in custody, the young man always insisted on his innocence. He gave the following reasons for his false confession:

1. The police kept on and on at him; he thought they would carry on questioning forever.
2. He desperately wanted the questioning to stop and felt very tired.
3. He claimed to have been hit on the head with a book by the senior detective and remained frightened of the police throughout the interviews.
4. At first he was determined not to give in to the police but after a while he lost his sense of control over the situation and eventually gave the police what he thought they wanted to hear. (Gudjonsson & MacKeith, 1990, p. 333)

He later stated that at no point during the interrogations did he come to believe that he had committed the crimes with which he was charged. A year later another man was charged with the crimes and pled guilty. His self-incriminating admissions were supported by other evidence.

(Source: Gudjonsson & MacKeith, 1990)

Were such "confessions" internalized, or were they mostly examples of the coerced-compliant category? Evidence suggests the latter, as we shall see soon.

More central to that aspect of the coerced-compliant category emphasizing private beliefs in the research of Edgar Schein and his colleagues (Schein, 1956; Schein, Schneier, & Barker, 1961) that documented how POWs coded hidden meanings into the messages they were forced to communicate. For example, Schein shows how the POWs were able to communicate their lack of repentance by the creative use of idiom and slang, such as emphasizing the wrong words in an apology. Example: "I am sorry I called Comrade Wong *a no-good son of a bitch*" (Schein, 1956, p. 159).

A clever example from an American POW in the Vietnam War was a naval aviator, Commander Jeremiah A. Denton, Jr. Paraded before television cameras in the spring of 1966 so that the North Vietnamese could "prove" their humane treatment of POWs, Denton described how well he was being treated, but at the same time he blinked the "torture" in Morse code with his eyelids (Fleming & Scott, 1991). Similarly, in the Gulf War, Air Force Major Jeffrey Tice used a fake accent when he read a statement prepared by his captors (Fleming & Scott, 1991).

Coerced-Internalized Confessions

At times, we are not aware that our response is being influenced by others; we assume it to be our independent judgment. Social psychologist Muzafer Sherif (1935) demonstrated the *autokinetic effect.* If you look at a stationary light in an otherwise completely dark room, the light will appear to move. Sherif capitalized on this phenomenon to study the effects of another person's response and found that a subject's reports of movements were highly influenced by other people's estimates, even without being aware of it.

It is also clear, similarly, that there are times when false confessions are *coerced-internalized,* that is, when the suspect—through the fatigue, pressures, and suggestiveness of the interrogation process—actually comes to believe that he or she committed the offense. Gudjonsson & MacKeith (1988) propose that coerced-compliant confessions are more easily elicited through aggressive interviewing techniques, whereas coerced-internalized confessions are produced by a more gently but relentlessly persuasive form of interviewing.

As an illustration of how a suspect might come to internalize the events as suggested by the police, consider the following case, described by Barthel (1976). Peter Reilly, 18 years old, returned home one night in 1973 to find that his mother had been murdered. He called the police who, after questioning him with the aid of a polygraph, began to suspect the boy of matricide. Transcripts of the interrogation sessions during a 25-hour period revealed a fascinating transition from denial through confusion and self-doubt (largely facilitated by the police officer's assertions about the infallibility of "the charts"), and finally to the statement, "well, it really looks like I did it" and the signing of a written statement—a rather ambiguous one, at that—of his responsibilities for the crime. Two years later, after Peter Reilly had been sentenced to prison, it was revealed through independent evidence that Reilly could not have committed the murder, that the confession even he came to believe was false.

More and more examples of internalized false confessions are coming to light. In a case described in more detail in Chapter 7, Paul Ingram—a deputy sheriff and an upstanding member of his community—confessed to a series of rapes and murders after being questioned by the police and a psychologist. Ingram became convinced that he had committed these acts, even though no other evidence supported such a conclusion.

Such pseudo-memories have mainly come to light as proposed explanations for some claims by adults that they were sexually abused when they were children. Do such long-repressed "memories" reflect what really happened? Some experimental psychologists who do research on memory and suggestibility argue that "the eagerness of therapists to uncover abuse, and their reliance on methods like hypnosis, can create imagined memories that the patients gradually assume to be fact" (Goleman, 1992, p. B5).

Elizabeth Loftus is an advocate of this perspective; in a preliminary study presented at the convention of the American Psychological Association, Loftus (1992) reported that she was able by suggestion to persuade people to remember details of an imaginary incident when they were supposedly lost at age 5, while their family was shopping. The subjects were two children and three adults; all came to believe the description, by a relative, of a fictitious fourth event along with three events that actually did happen to them.

PSYCHOLOGICAL PERSPECTIVES

Various theories have been brought to bear on the question "What is it about the coerciveness of interrogation that can cause innocent people to incriminate themselves?" From a psychological standpoint, the coerced-compliant false confessions are readily explained by the individual's desire to escape an aversive situation and secure a favorable self-outcome. In these cases, the act of confession—compared to the consequences of silence or denial—is simply the lesser of two evils for a beleaguered suspect. But what about the more puzzling instances of internalized false confessions?

Interrogation as a Hypnotic State

To account for this phenomenon, some observers have likened the interrogation process to hypnosis (Ofshe, 1992). Foster (1969), referring to the "station house syndrome," stated that police interrogation "can produce a trance-like state of heightened suggestibility" so that "truth and falsehood become hopelessly confused in the suspect's mind" (pp. 690-691). Because the state of hypnosis is characterized by the subject's loss of initiative, heightened capacity for fantasy production, confabulation and reality distortion (e.g., an acceptance of falsified memories), and an increased suggestibility (e.g., in response to leading questions; see Hilgard, 1975), the danger of what appear to be internalized false confessions could provide a real source of concern. Indeed, a study by Weinstein, Abrams, and Gibbons (1970) revealed that when a false sense of guilt is implanted in hypnotized subjects, they become less able to pass a polygraphic lie detector test.

Interestingly, almost a century ago, Hugo Münsterberg (1908) reported on a murder case in which the defendant was convicted on the basis of a confession that might have been elicited through hypnotic induction. In 1906, a woman named Bessie Hollister was raped and murdered. Richard Ivens discovered the body and immediately reported it to the police. He was questioned intensively and eventually confessed to the crime, although he later repudiated his confession and had an unimpeachable alibi.

What, then, prompted the sudden shift during interrogation from denial to confession? According to Ivens, his only recollection of the session was of seeing a revolver pointed at him—"I saw the flash of steel in front of me. Then two men got before me. I can remember no more than that about it. . . . I suppose I must have made those statements, since they all say I did. But I have no knowledge of having made them" (Münsterberg, 1908, pp. 168-170). As it turned out, the defense sought the opinion of several experts as to whether the confession could be explained through the use of hypnosis. Affirmative replies were received from many sources, including Hugo Münsterberg and William James, but they were disregarded and the young man was executed.

Interrogative Suggestibility

The essence of the hypnotic state is, in our opinion, its extreme suggestibility. Gudjonsson and Clark (1986) have developed the concept of *interrogative suggestibility* to explain individual differences in responses to police questioning. They define interrogative suggestibility as "the extent to which within a closed social interaction, people come to accept messages communicated during formal questioning, as the result of which their subsequent behavioral response is affected" (Gudjonsson, 1991, p. 280).

Five interrelated components are part of the concept:

1. a closed social interaction between the interrogator and the interviewee;
2. a questioning procedure that involves two or more participants;
3. a suggestive stimulus;
4. acceptance of the suggestive stimulus; and
5. a behavioral response to indicate whether or not the suggestion is accepted (Gudjonsson, 1991).

Interrogative suggestibility, according to Gudjonsson (1986, 1989), differs from other types of suggestibility in four ways: the above-mentioned closed nature of the social interaction, the questions dealing with past experiences and recollections, its inclusion of a component of uncertainty, and its stressful situation with important consequences for the person being interviewed. In this situation, the interrogator can manipulate three aspects—uncertainty, interpersonal trust, and expectation—to alter the person's susceptibility to suggestions.

But characteristics of the interviewee also affect the process; as an instance, the type of coping strategy used during the interview affects his or her level of suggestibility.

For example, avoidance coping is likely to facilitate a suggestible response whereby people give answers that to them seem plausible and consistent with the external clues provided, rather than only giving definite answers to questions they clearly remember. In contrast, a nonsuggestible coping strategy involves a critical analysis of the situation and a facilitative problem-solving action. (Gudjonsson, 1991, p. 282)

Furthermore, people who are suspicious are less suggestible than those with a trusting cognitive set; those with poor memories and low intelligence are generally more suggestible; and low self-esteem, lack of assertiveness, and anxiety affect suggestibility. Gudjonsson (1984b) has developed a suggestibility scale (the Gudjonsson Suggestibility Scale [GSS]) and a parallel form (Gudjonsson, 1987) to assess subjects' responses to leading questions and negative feedback. It uses a narrative paragraph describing a fictitious mugging, which is read to the subjects. They are then asked to recall all they can about the story. After a delay of about 50 minutes, the subject is asked 20 specific questions, 15 of which are subtly misleading. After answering these, the person is informed that he or she has made a number of mistakes (even if no errors have been made), and thus it is necessary to ask each of the questions once more. The person is instructed to try to be more accurate than before. Any change in answers from the previous trial is labeled a "shift"; the extent to which people give in to the misleading questions is scored as a "yield." "Yield" and "shift" are added together to make up a "total suggestibility" score (Gudjonsson, 1991). Interestingly, these two measures are not highly correlated and load on different factors (Gudjonsson, 1984b). The GSS measure of interrogative suggestibility appears to be independent of hypnotizability (Gudjonsson, 1986).

It is possible to manipulate the expectations of subjects prior to interrogation in order to reduce or enhance suggestibility as measured by the suggestibility scale (Gudjonsson & Hilton, 1989; Hansdottir, Thorsteinsson, Kristinsdottir, & Ragnarsson, 1990). Furthermore, interrogative suggestibility has been found to be significantly related to the coping strategy that subjects report using during the test (Gudjonsson, 1988). Those subjects who were most suggestible tended to use an avoidance coping strategy during the interrogation. Gudjonsson (1991) observes that this means that "they failed to be able to evaluate each question critically and give answers that to them seemed plausible and consistent with the external cues provided. Nonsuggestible subjects, on the other hand, were able to adopt a critical analysis of the situation which facilitated the accuracy of their answers" (p. 285).

Interrogative suggestibility appears to be mediated by anxiety; scores on the GSS are correlated with state anxiety as measured by the Spielberger State-Trait Anxiety Inventory. Subjects who gave in most to the interrogative pressures were those who rated themselves as being most anxious at the time (Gudjonsson, 1988).

The ultimate validity of the proposal that individual differences in interrogative suggestibility affect behavior during questioning would be a test with actual criminal suspects. Three studies have made a comparison between two groups of such suspects: those who were able to resist police interrogation pressures in spite of some salient evidence against them, and those who made a self-incriminating confession that they subsequently retracted.

The first (Gudjonsson, 1984a) compared the suggestibility scores of 12 alleged false confessors and 8 resisters; the latter group was found to be significantly more intelligent and less suggestible than the alleged false confessors. In a similar study using a larger sample, Gudjonsson (1990) compared 100 alleged false confessors with 104 other criminal defendants charged with similar offenses. (All had been referred to psychologists for evaluation.) The mean ages for the two groups were 29 and 34, respectively. The average IQ of the alleged false confessors was 80.0, significantly less than the average of 91.4 for the comparison group. The alleged false confessors scored significantly higher on measures of suggestibility, compliance, and acquiescence. The third study compared the suggestibility scores of 20 resisters and 20 alleged false confessors who were matched for age, sex, intelligence level, memory recall capacity, and the seriousness of the offense (Gudjonsson, 1991). The two groups differed quite clearly in suggestibility. "The ability of the suspect to cope with interroga-tive pressure is more important than his or her tendency to give in to leading questions per se" (p. 286).

The next step beyond suggestibility, as reflected in this program of work, is compliance. Gudjonsson (1990) differentiates between suggestibility and compliance by noting that the latter does not require an internal acceptance of the request. We earlier described the term *coerced-compliant* confessions similarly; the individual makes a conscious decision to carry out the behavior, whether or not he or she has agreed with it privately. Some of the mediating vari-ables—eagerness to please, avoidance of controversy—are common to both suggestibility and compliance (Gudjonsson & Clark, 1986).

Gudjonsson has constructed a brief true-false scale to measure compliance; the items are listed in Box 5.2.

Self-Perception Theory

From another standpoint, it has been suggested that internalized false confessions could result from a process of self-perception. Interested in "When saying is believing," Bem (1966) explored the idea that a false confession could distort an individual's recall of his or her own past behavior if the confession is emitted in the presence of cues previously associated with telling the truth (e.g., reassurance that one need not admit to wrongdoing). In an interesting experiment, subjects performed a task that required them to cross out a sample of words from a master list. Then, to establish two lights as discriminative stimuli for truth and falsity, subjects were asked general questions about themselves and instructed to answer them truthfully when the room was illuminated by a green light and to lie in the presence of an amber light. In the next phase of the procedure, the experimenter announced several words taken from the initial task. After some words he instructed subjects to lie and after others to tell the truth about whether they had previously crossed the word out— again while in the presence of a green or amber light.

In the final step of the procedure, subjects were asked, for each word, to recall whether they actually had or had not crossed it out. The results indicated that false statements made in the presence of the truth light produced more errors in the recall of actual performance than either false statements made in the presence of the lie light or none at all. It thus appears that under conditions normally associated with telling the truth, subjects came to believe the lies they had been induced to tell. In discussing the legal implications of this finding, Bem (1967) noted that "a physical or emotional rubber hose never convinced anyone of anything" and that "saying becomes believing only when we feel the presence of truth, and certainly only when a minimum of inducement and the mildest and most subtle forms of coercion are used" (pp. 23-24).

Generalization from Bem's laboratory research to the real-world process of criminal interrogation should obviously be made with

BOX 5.2
Gudjonsson's Compliance Items

1. I give in easily to people when I am pressured.
2. I find it very difficult to tell people when I disagree with them.
3. People in authority make me feel uncomfortable and uneasy.
4. I tend to give in to people who insist they are right.
5. I tend to become easily alarmed and frightened when I am in the company of people of authority.
6. I try very hard not to offend people in authority.
7. I would describe myself as a very obedient person.
8. I tend to go along with what people tell me even when I know that they are wrong.
9. I believe in avoiding rather than facing demanding and frightening situations.
10. I try to please others.
11. Disagreeing with people often takes more time than it is worth.
12. I generally believe in doing as I am told.
13. When I am uncertain about things I tend to accept what people tell me.
14. I generally try to avoid confrontation with people.
15. As a child I always did what my parents told me.
16. I try hard to do what is expected of me.
*17. I am not too concerned about what people think of me.
*18. I strongly resist being pressured to do things I don't want to do.
*19. I would never go along with what people tell me in order to please them.
20. When I was a child I sometimes took the blame for things I had not done.

*Item is worded in opposite direction.

(Adapted from Gudjonsson, 1990, p. 540.)

caution. Still, anecdotal reports suggest the existence of internalized false confessions, and Bem's self-perception ideas provide at least a partial explanation of this phenomenon. Closely related, for example, is an interrogation tactic described by Driver (1968) of having the suspect repeat the story over and over, for "if duped into playing the part of the criminal in an imaginary sociodrama, the suspect may come to believe that he was the central actor in the crime" (p. 53).

TRUE CONFESSIONS

The focus of this chapter has been on false confessions and the motives for them. But a large number of confessions reflect the truth as the confessor sees it. This section reviews psychological contributions to an understanding of the desire to reveal the truth.

Seeking Forgiveness

Several years ago, the media disclosed that Jimmy Swaggart, the television evangelist, had frequently availed himself of the services of a prostitute. Sobbing as he spoke, the Reverend Mr. Swaggart confessed to his followers, "I am a sinner." Surprisingly, this admission did not mean the end of his career. Some of his followers commended him for his confession, accepted his recognition of his frailties, and concluded that his confession would strengthen him. He was preaching again 6 months later.

Certainly one motivation for true confessions is to generate sympathy for the transgressor or forgiveness. A program of research by Weiner, Graham, Peter, and Zmuidinas (1991) found that confession had strong beneficial effects; that is, the confessor's personality and character were rated more favorably by others, especially when the person confessed before he or she was accused of any wrongdoing.

The Healing Power of Confessions

The beneficial quality of confession has a long tradition: The early Christians were told that by mutual confession and prayer they would be cleansed of all unrighteousness. Oscar Wilde wrote: "A man's very highest moment is, I have no doubt, when he kneels in the dust and beats his breast, and tells all the sins of his life" (quoted by Rogge, 1959, p. 209). Freud proposed that talking about traumas could cure depression, and a popular saying has it that "confession is good for the soul."

James W. Pennebaker (1987, 1990), a social psychologist, has sought to demonstrate the hypothesis that not only is confession good for the soul, but it benefits the body also. Over the last decade he has offered people an opportunity and a setting for opening up, a chance for people to confide in someone who is receptive, and confess their secrets—maybe for the first time. He has asked respondents about various childhood traumas they have experienced—everything from rape and molestation to the death or divorce of their parents. As might be expected, he finds that having experienced traumatic experiences in childhood is associated with increased physical illness in adulthood, with a higher incidence of everything from common colds and respiratory problems to ulcers, cancer, and heart problems. *But* talking about traumas that occurred during childhood serves to protect the adult's physical health. Confessing their secrets led to better outlooks for their physical health. Pennebaker equates these effects with the observation often made by professional polygraphers—that if a crime suspect eventually confesses, his or her biological stress levels drop—even though eventual punishment may be the result. He finds that disclosing personal traumas leads to an increased blood pressure during the disclosure, but then a dip in level of blood pressure even below the predisclosure level. Disclosure also improved immune system activity and status on other biological measures. In general, they felt better, had a more positive outlook, and exhibited a drop in medical complaints over the next 6 months. In summary, Pennebaker's studies indicate that confessing traumatic experiences can yield immediate physical benefits.

Theodore Reik's discussion, in *The Compulsion to Confess* (1959), takes this analysis a step further. All of us, he proposes, harbor deep-seated guilt feelings regarding our real or imagined transgressions during childhood. Guilt is best relieved by confession (along with punishment and absolution) so, according to Reik, the need to confess is present to some degree in each of us.

The call-in-a-confession "hot line" in Los Angeles verifies Reik's claim. Started in 1988, confession hot lines are telephone numbers that people may call to disclose their deepest secrets. Pennebaker (1990) reports that the Los Angeles hotline gets two hundred confessions per day.

SIX

Jurors' Reactions to Confessions Evidence

Michael D. Peterson was a transient who panhandled around the Kansas City area. In 1983 he was charged with the murder of a volunteer librarian at a Christian Science reading room in a Kansas City suburb. The prosecution presented a videotape of the defendant confessing to the crime, in which he calmly admitted that he shot the victim with a .22-caliber handgun after she refused his demand for small change. But the defendant took the stand to claim that this "confession" had been coerced as a result of physical and verbal harassment. His defense attorney introduced a second tape recording, made 2 days after the first, in which Peterson recanted the confession, telling two police detectives that he had been forced to confess and that he had an alibi; he was, he said, in a different county, with friends, on the day of the murder. Given the two conflicting tapes, which would jurors believe? Would they conclude that the confession was, in fact, a voluntary one, or would they believe that it had been coerced? Their verdict would be immeasurably influenced by this decision.

Chapter 2 described the decision by the U.S. Supreme Court in the 1972 *Lego v. Twomey* case, the important decision that justified a lower standard by which the fact finder may admit a confession whose voluntariness had been in question. Is the Court's assumption well founded; do jurors discount a possibly coerced confession? A program of research we have carried out over the past decade questions the validity of this assumption. This chapter reports several research findings; the procedures and results of our studies are described in some detail.

Although no prior research existed bearing directly on how jurors use information about a coerced confession, when we began our studies the cognitive process involved in such a decision was familiar to attribution researchers. (Attribution theory is described in Chapter 5.) Jurors are, after all, confronted with a behavior whose cause is ambiguous. If a defendant confesses while under threat during interrogation, that confession may be viewed either as reflecting the defendant's actual guilt or as the person's way of avoiding the negative consequences of remaining silent. Ideally, jurors who employ the attributional principle of discounting (Kelley, 1971) would be less confident about the truth and reliability of this type of elicited confession than they would about one that is made in the absence of threat as a plausible cause.

Despite the compelling logic of discounting, researchers have found that when people explain the behavior of others, they tend to underestimate the impact of situations, and overestimate the role of personal factors. This bias is so pervasive and often so misleading that it has been called the *fundamental attribution error* (Ross, 1977).

The fundamental attribution error was first discovered by Jones and Harris (1967). In a series of experiments, these investigators had subjects either read an essay expressing a viewpoint or hear a speech presumably written by another student. In one of their studies, subjects read an essay in which the communicator either supported or criticized the unpopular Castro regime in Cuba. Some subjects were told that the communicator had freely chosen to advocate this position (called the choice condition), whereas others were told that the communicator had been assigned to endorse the unpopular position by a political-science instructor (the no-choice condition). Results indicated that the subjects in the no-choice condition clearly perceived that the communicator's expressed opinion had been determined by the situation, that is, the instructions from the political science instructor. Nevertheless, their impressions about the communicator's true beliefs were markedly influenced by the particular position he had espoused. Subjects thus did not dismiss the dispositional cause of a situationally determined opinion. This finding has been repeated many times. Whether the essay topic is nuclear power, abortion, drug laws, or the death penalty, the results are essentially the same (Jones, 1990). In fact, people fall prey to the fundamental attribution error even when they are fully aware of the situation's impact on behavior. In one study, the subjects were themselves assigned to take a position, whereupon they swapped essays and rated each other. Remarkably, they still jumped to conclusions about each other's attitudes (Miller, Jones, & Hinkle, 1981). In another study, subjects inferred attitudes from a speech even when they were the ones who assigned the position to be taken (Gilbert & Jones, 1986). Logic aside, people are quick to take what someone says at face value and assume that it reflects on his or her personal dispositions.

The parallels between this research and the predicament of evaluating coerced confessions, elicited in an interrogation, are striking. In both, the observer is faced with a verbal behavior that he or she may attribute either to the behaver's true attitude or to the pressures of the situation. Yet, even though the U.S. Supreme Court assumed that jurors would reject an involuntary confession as unreliable and hence not let it guide their decisions, social psychological research suggests that jurors might not totally reject the confession when considering the behaver's true guilt. Thus we initiated a series of experiments to evaluate these divergent predictions.

But to complicate matters even further, the legal system defines coercion in two ways—as either a *threat* of harm and punishment or as a *promise* of leniency and immunity from prosecution. Both are viewed by the Court as equivalent conditions for determining involuntariness. In fact, jurors are sometimes provided with this legal definition as a part of the judge's instructions.

The problem differs from state to state, however. Many states have used what is known as the "orthodox rule"—once the judge decides to admit a confession, the voluntariness issue is never introduced to the jury. Consequently, jurors—like the subjects in the initial study we will describe—do not receive any special instructions on the matter. But—and here matters become less problematic—many states do provide that after confession evidence is admitted, the judge must instruct the jury to decide the issue of voluntariness before rendering a verdict. In states employing this latter procedure, two types of instruction are available: (a) a short form, which simply asks jurors to determine voluntariness and reject any confession that is coerced; and (b) a long form that additionally defines *coercion* as either a positive or negative inducement and explains the reasons for its unreliability.

The relevant portion of the short form reads:

If the evidence in the case does not convince you beyond a reasonable doubt that a confession was made voluntarily and intentionally, the jury should disregard it entirely. On the other hand, if the evidence in the case does show beyond a reasonable doubt that a confession was in fact voluntarily and intentionally made by a defendant, the jury should consider it as evidence in the case against the defendant who voluntarily and intentionally made the confession. (Mathes & DeVitt, 1965, p. 101)

The longer version adds the following:

If it appears from the evidence in the case that a confession would not have been made, but for some threat of harm or some offer of promise or immunity from prosecution, or leniency in punishment, or other reward, such a confession should not be considered as having been voluntarily made, because of the danger that a person accused might be persuaded by the pressure of hope or fear to confess as facts things which are not true, in an effort to avoid threatened harm or punishment, or to secure a promised reward. (Mathes & DeVitt, 1965, p. 103)

The courts may treat a threat of punishment and a promise of leniency as equivalent (i.e., as both coercive), but research suggests that people attribute more responsibility and freedom to a person for actions taken to gain a positive outcome than for similar actions aimed at avoiding punishment. Kruglanski and Cohen (1974) tested a variant of this hypothesis and found that a person who chose between two unattractive alternatives was viewed as having a lower freedom of choice than one who chose between one attractive and one unattractive alternative. The implications of these findings for how jurors might utilize different types of coerced confessions are clear. Specifically, they suggest that a confession that is made under coercive influence of a promise of leniency (positive constraint) will be perceived by jurors to be more voluntary and hence as more indicative of guilt than one that followed a threat of punishment (negative constraint). Accordingly, we initiated an experiment (Kassin & Wrightsman, 1980, Experiment 1) that incorporated two versions of a coerced confession—one in which the admission was made in response to the offer of a positive outcome and one in which it followed the threat of a negative outcome.

A 25-page trial transcript was read by 64 subjects. The defendant, Ron Oliver, was charged with transporting a stolen car across state lines. Generally stated, the government's case was based on the testimony of a used car salesman, who identified Ronald Oliver as the person who stole the car from the lot, and the statement of a highway patrolman, who stopped the defendant for speeding and subsequently made the arrest. The defendant, on the other hand, maintained that he was driving an acquaintance's car and had no knowledge that the vehicle had been stolen. The transcript thus consisted of opening statements by counsel, examination of two prosecution witnesses (the salesman from whom the car was stolen and the arresting officer) and one defense witness (the defendant), closing arguments, and the judge's instruction to the jury. The judge's charge was brief and very general; it merely reiterated the accusation, outlined the jury's duties, and explicated the requirements of proof (i.e., that the defendant is presumed innocent and that the prosecution must prove guilt beyond a reasonable doubt). No mention was made of the confession or the issue of voluntariness.

The four versions of the transcript given to different subjects were identical except for the inclusion of testimony that indicated that after the officer informed the defendant that he was under arrest for stealing the car, Ron Oliver confessed.

In the *confession-no constraint* condition, Ron Oliver confessed immediately after he was accused of stealing the car. In the *confession-promise* condition, he first denied the crime, but after the police officer told him that if he confessed, he would be treated well during his detention and the judge would be easier on him, Oliver admitted he stole the car. The third condition, the *confession-threat* condition, had the police officer react to an initial denial by telling Oliver that he would be treated more harshly during the detention and by the judge; he then confessed. In the *no confession* condition, the defendant denied stealing the car; the police officer did not offer any inducements to confess.

The main dependent variables in Experiment 1 were a verdict (guilty-not guilty), an estimate of the probability that the defendant committed the crime (0%-100%, in multiples of 5), and ratings of the extent to which subjects' decisions were influenced by the testimony of each witness.

Only 22 subjects voted guilty (34%) whereas 43 voted not guilty (66%). An inspection of verdicts in the four groups revealed conviction rates of 56% in the confession-no constraint group, 38% in the confession-promise group, 25% in the confession-threat group, and 19% in the no-confession group. The overall difference among groups, however, only approached statistical significance. A scalar variable was defined by combining subjects' verdicts with their 0-8 confidence ratings (confidence itself was unaffected by the independent variable). As with the above analysis, a one-way analysis of variance on these verdict-confidence scores indicated that the differences among the four groups were only marginally significant.

After rendering a verdict and confidence rating, subjects indicated the likelihood that the defendant committed the crime by circling a number from 0 to 100. In contrast to the judgmental data, these probability-of-commission estimates were significantly affected by the confession manipulation. In particular, the defendant was viewed as more likely to have committed the crime when he confessed without external constraint ($M = 65\%$), or when he confessed in response to a promise of leniency ($M = 55\%$), than when no confession ($M = 30\%$) was made. The confession-threat manipulation produced a relatively moderate probability-of-commission ($M = 47\%$) that tended to be lower than the estimate in the confession-no constraint group.

In summary, information about a prior confession and its surrounding circumstances influenced subjects' estimates of the likelihood that the defendant committed the crime. Some interesting differences emerged on this measure. First, the absolute probative value of a retracted confession was demonstrated by the fact that probability-of-commission estimates were significantly higher in the confession-no constraint group than in the no-confession group. Beyond that, the positive and negative constraints did not produce equivalent results. Compared to the no-confession group, subjects' beliefs about the defendant's culpability were significantly increased by a confession that was elicited by a positive offer but not by one that was elicited by a threat. The potential danger of admitting the former as evidence is thus apparent.

Two major shortcomings deserve mention. First, the differences cited above were obtained for subjects' probability-of-commission estimates, but not for the practically important variable—verdicts. This failure to obtain differences in verdict could have resulted from the fact that the case against the defendant was weak (note that the mean probability-of-commission estimate was only 49%) and did not permit enough variability in judgments (see Kerr et al., 1976). Second, we can only infer that the probability-of-commission differences were mediated by perceived choice because the latter variable was not directly assessed. Therefore, we conducted a second study with the following goals in mind: to replicate the probability-of-commission findings using a stronger (i.e., pro-prosecution) version of the case, to determine whether this increase in probability-of-commission would produce a confession-constraint effect on verdicts, and to measure perceived choice directly.

In our second experiment (Kassin & Wrightsman, 1981), 72 subjects were randomly assigned to one of the four groups. Stylistically and substantively, the transcript was very similar to the one employed in the first experiment. A number of changes were made in order to bolster the prosecutor's case against the defendant, and the revised transcript was 22 pages in length. The portion of testimony that contained the confession manipulation and the experimental procedure was identical to that of the first experiment. In order to determine the efficacy of the changes that were made, the resultant transcript was pretested. Specifically, this revised version of the no-confession case was distributed to 10 subjects who provided probability-of-commission estimates. Compared to the control group in Experiment 1 (M = 30%), the mean probability-of-commission estimate for this version was 44%.

In addition to the dependent variables assessed in the first study, subjects indicated the standard of proof they thought was necessary for conviction by answering, "The defendant should be found guilty if there is at least a _% chance that he committed the crime." After rendering their verdicts and answering the remaining questions, subjects in the experimental (confession) groups also indicated whether the confession was voluntary and how confident they were in that decision. The results are presented in Table 6.1.

PROBABILITY-OF-COMMISSION ESTIMATES

A major goal of the second study was to increase the perceived probability that the defendant committed the crime in order to produce greater variability in verdicts. This goal was achieved, as the overall mean probability-of-commission estimate was 58% (compared to 49% in Experiment 1).

Moreover, the pattern of group differences was the same as those produced in the first experiment. Estimates were highest in the no-constraint confession group and lowest in the no-confession control group. Further tests revealed that the positive constraint produced probability-of-commission estimates that were higher than those of the control groups and not significantly different from those obtained in the no-constraint condition. On the other hand, the estimates of negative-constraint subjects were lower than in the no-constraint group and not significantly different from those obtained in the control group (see Table 6.1).

Verdicts

Overall, 29 of the 72 subjects (40%) rendered guilty verdicts, and the difference among groups was highly significant. Specifically, the proportion of guilty verdicts was highest in the no-constraint confession group (78%) and lowest in the control group (11%). The proportion of guilty verdicts in the negative-constraint group (22%) was

TABLE 6.1
Effects of Confession Conditions, Experiment 2

Scalar Variables	Experimental (Confession Groups) (percentage)			Control (No Confession Group) (percentage)
	No Constraint	Positive Constraint	Negative Constraint	
Verdicts: voting guilty	78.0	50.0	22.0	11.0
Probability-of-commission	76.67	63.33	51.39	40.28
Reasonable doubt	85.56	82.28	85.94	92.22
Voluntariness judgments	94.0	39.0	22.0	not asked

significantly lower than in the no-constraint group and equivalent (i.e., not significantly different) to those in the control group. Yet, the confession that was elicited by a positive offer produced a greater proportion of guilty verdicts (50%) than in the control group and was not significantly different from the no-constraint condition.

An analysis of the verdict-confidence scores also indicated a significant difference among groups and a pattern that closely paralleled the judgmental data.

Reasonable Doubt

Recall that the subjects defined their standards of reasonable doubt by answering the question, "The defendant should be found guilty if there is at least a _% chance that he committed the crime." Interestingly, the overall estimate of reasonable doubt was 86%, which is almost identical to that previously found using a videotape of the Ron Oliver case (Kassin & Wrightsman, 1979) and to that initially reported by Simon and Mahan (1971). No group differences emerged on this variable; presumably, the obtained differences in verdict followed from differences along the probability-of-commission dimension and not from an increase or decrease in the standards set for conviction.

Voluntariness Judgments

Subjects in the three experimental groups judged whether or not the defendant had confessed voluntarily and without coercion, and then indicated their confidence in these decisions. As it turned out, voluntariness judgments were significantly affected by the circumstances surrounding the confession. Subsequent tests indicated a greater percentage of voluntariness judgments in the no-constraint group (94%) than in either the positive (39%) or negative (22%) constraint groups, which, in turn, did not significantly differ from each other. As with the verdicts, a scaler variable was defined by assigning positive confidence values to "voluntary" and negative values to "involuntary" judgments. A significant difference among groups corroborated the judgmental data—the confession was seen as more voluntary in the no-constraint group than in the positive or negative constraint conditions (see Table 6.1). Thus, although the negative and no-constraint groups responded in the predicted manner, results for the positive-constraint group were surprising. Quite unexpectedly, these latter subjects acknowledged that the confession that influenced their verdicts was involuntary and coerced.

Let us recapitulate. Two interrelated points of dispute between the legal system's assumptions and the psychological literature on social perception were addressed in these first two experiments. First, the Supreme Court's presumption that jurors can accurately assess the truthfulness of confessions is challenged by research that suggests that observers often accept a situationally caused statement or behavior at face value. Second, the legal definition of a coerced confession as one that is prompted by either an offer or a threat conflicts with the finding that observers phenomenologically treat the positive and negative constraints very differently.

In these first two experiments, the prediction that jurors would discount a coerced confession as unreliable was only partially supported and must be qualified by reference to Bramel's (1969) and Kelley's (1971) hypotheses about perceived choice. When the coercive influence was operationally defined as a threat of harm or punishment, subjects clearly discounted the confession evidence—

they viewed the confession as involuntary and manifested a relatively low rate of conviction. However, when coercion took the form of an offer or a promise of leniency, subjects were unable or unwilling to dismiss the prior confession. Under these circumstances, subjects conceded that the defendant had confessed involuntarily, but voted guilty anyway. Consistent with previous research (Jones & Harris, 1967), then, the defendant's behavior was accepted as probative despite the presence and perception of a positive constraint. At this point, a theoretically meaningful ambiguity in the interpretation of these results deserves mention. Specifically, it is possible that the differences obtained between the *kinds* of constraint (i.e., positive vs. negative) were, in fact, related to differences in the perceived *degree* of cause. Wells (1980) has found that people often erroneously assume that punishment is a more powerful form of behavioral inducement than is a reward contingency. In the present study, subjects may thus have accepted the positively constrained confession not because the constraint was positive per se, but because it was perceived as being a relatively weak inducement. This alternative interpretation is refuted only indirectly by the fact that in Experiment 2, voluntariness judgments in the positive and negative constraint groups were not statistically different. Admittedly, however, equally frequent recognition of some constraint does not mean an equivalence in the perceived degrees of constraint.

The generalizability of the present study is an issue that merits some discussion. Although the internal consistency and replicability of results within the employed paradigm have been amply demonstrated, the external validity of these experiments is limited by the fact that we assessed the judgments of individual, nondeliberating subjects. Some might propose that questions about the reliability of evidence would arise during group discussion and serve to decrease jurors' use of a positively induced confession. Kaplan and Miller (1978) have concluded that jury discussion may correct for certain pretrial and midtrial biases. But in an opposite direction are the results of a study on the effects of pretrial publicity by Kramer, Kerr, and Carroll (1990) who found that jury deliberation accentuated the impact of pretrial publicity, despite admonitions that it should not be considered.

In view of the fact that, as we noted in Chapter 1, disputed confessions arise in approximately 20% of all criminal cases, the problem addressed here is a real one. What then, are the practical implications of these results? The present findings suggest that perhaps the courts should explicitly distinguish between positive and negative forms of coercion (or among varying degrees of coercion) and exercise caution when admitting the former as evidence. Toward this end, at least two types of safeguard could be implemented within current regulations. First, the state courts could, at their discretion, require a stringent standard of proof (e.g., proof beyond a reasonable doubt) by which to determine at pretrial hearings the voluntariness and hence admissibility of a prior confession. Alternatively, a judicial instruction could serve as the vehicle by which to correct jurors' biases.

Indeed, some states (e.g., Massachusetts) advocate that even after a judge has admitted a confession as evidence, he or she must instruct the jurors that they too should decide the voluntariness issue before rendering a verdict. On the negative side, many legal scholars (Frank, 1949; Kalven & Zeisel, 1966) and researchers (Sue, Smith, & Caldwell, 1973) have observed that judges' instructions often have little impact on jury decisions. In fact, some investigators have reported a "boomerang effect" whereby jurors who are admonished to ignore a critical piece of inadmissible evidence attach *greater* weight to that testimony than do those who are not so instructed (Broeder, 1959; Wolf & Montgomery, 1977).

A third experiment (Kassin & Wrightsman, 1981) was thus designed with three goals in mind—to replicate earlier results, to test the effects of two ecologically valid forms of judicial instruction, and to measure directly whether the positive and negative types of coercion differ in the perceived strength of their inducement value. Accordingly, subjects acting as mock jurors read the transcript of the Ronald Oliver trial; again, testimony revealed either that the accused person had confessed to the arresting officer on his own initiative, or in response to an offer of leniency, or in response to a threat of punishment. Subjects also received from the judge a brief confession-related instruction, the more detailed instruction that tried to define "voluntary," or no instruction at all. Afterwards, subjects judged the voluntariness of the confession, rendered their verdicts, and answered other case-related questions (see also Box 6.1.)

When all subjects in a session had completed their reading of the trial transcript, they filled out a questionnaire individually and without deliberation. On it, experimental (i.e., confession) subjects first made a voluntariness judgment by answering, "Did Ron Oliver confess to Patrolman Matheson voluntarily and without coercion— yes or no?" and then indicated their confidence in that decision. Next, all subjects rendered their verdicts and indicated their confidence associated with that response. Note that voluntariness judgments always preceded verdicts in order to simulate the decision order that real jurors are faced with. Subjects then answered a number of other case-related questions. Specifically, they estimated the probability that the defendant had committed the crime and the standard of proof they thought was necessary for conviction (i.e., "In this case, the defendant should be found guilty if there is at least a % chance that he committed the crime"), and they rated the extent to which their verdicts were influenced by the three witnesses' testimony and the judge's closing instruction. Finally, to test whether the positive and negative constraints were perceived to differ in strength of inducement, experimental subjects rated "How much pressure did Patrolman Matheson exert on Ron Oliver to confess?"

Verdicts

Overall, the stimulus trial in Experiment 3 elicited a perfect split in verdicts—85 subjects (50%) voted guilty and 85 (50%) voted not guilty. The conviction rates were 63% (32/51) in the no-constraint condition, 51% (26/51) in the positive-constraint condition, and 41% (21/51) in the negative-constraint condition. This difference between conditions was not quite significant. The instruction manipulation had no effect on verdicts.

In order to obtain a more sensitive between-groups comparison, a scalar variable was once more generated by combining subjects' verdicts with their confidence levels. Paralleling the dichotomous data, an analysis of variance on these scores revealed a significant

BOX 6.1
Judge's Instructions on Voluntariness

Some evolution has occurred in regard to the approved instructions to the jury regarding confessions. Recent federal jury instructions (Devitt, Blackmar, Wolff, & O'Malley, 1987) include the following:

> Evidence relating to any alleged statement, confessions, admission, or act or omission alleged to have been made or done by a defendant outside of court and after a crime has been committed should always be considered by the jury with caution and weighed with great care. All such alleged statements, confessions, or admissions should be disregarded entirely unless the other evidence in the case convinces the jury beyond a reasonable doubt that the statement, confession, admission, or act or omission was made or done knowingly and voluntarily.
>
> In determining whether any statement, confession, admission, or act or omission alleged to have been made by a defendant outside of court and after a crime has been committed was knowingly and voluntarily made or done, the jury should consider the age, training, education, occupation, and physical and mental condition of the defendant, and [his] [her] treatment while in custody or under interrogation as shown by the evidence in the case. Also consider all other circumstances in evidence surrounding the making of the statement, confession, or admission.
>
> If after considering the evidence you determine that a statement, confession, admission, or act or omission was made or done knowingly and voluntarily, you may give it such weight as you feel is deserves under the circumstances. (p. 411)

More radically, the Committee on Model Jury Instructions for the Ninth Circuit Court of Appeals (1992) has advocated the use of *statement* rather than *confession;* the latter is considered too pejorative or prejudicial. They propose:

> You have heard testimony that the defendant made a statement. It is for you to decide (1) whether defendant made the statement and (2) if so, how much weight to give it. In making these decisions, you should consider all of the evidence about the statement, including the circumstances under which the defendant may have made it. (p. 51)

main effect for confession condition. Specifically, subjects were less likely to vote confidently for conviction in the negative-constraint condition than in the no-constraint condition. The positive inducement fell between these extremes.

The instruction manipulation had no effect either alone or in interaction with constraint type on these verdict-confidence scores. It did, however, have a significant effect on confidence per se. That is, subjects were generally more confident in their verdicts when they received the short-form instruction than no instruction at all. The long-form instruction did not differ significantly from either of these conditions.

Voluntariness Judgments

Overall, 66 out of the 153 experimental subjects (42%) judged the defendant's confession to be voluntary. Over levels of instruction, the percentages of "voluntary" judgments were 73% (37/51) under no constraint, 37% (19/51) under positive constraint, and 20% (10/51) under negative constraint. The overall difference among groups was highly significant. Subsequent chi squared analyses revealed that more voluntariness judgments were made under no constraint than positive constraint, which, in turn, produced more voluntariness judgments than the negative constraint. Again, the judge's instruction did not have a significant impact.

As before, a scalar variable was created by combining subjects' voluntariness judgments with their 0-8 confidence levels. An analysis of these scores corroborated the pattern of results for the dichotomous decisions. A main effect for constraint condition showed that the defendant's confession was seen as more voluntary when given in the absence of any inducement than under positive or negative constraints. As in the earlier studies, the positive inducement was seen as significantly more voluntary than the negative one. Again, the judge's instruction played no role in these decisions.

Experiment 3 provided some interesting insights into the impact that a pretrial confession has on potential jurors. At the most basic level, a comparison of verdicts in the no-confession control group with those in the confession/no-constraint condition reaffirms the time-honored suspicion that evidence about a prior confession is often sufficient to elicit a conviction. More important, these results replicate very closely those obtained in Experiments 1 and 2. When confronted with a defendant who had confessed in response to a threat of harm or punishment, subjects clearly discounted the confession. In line with the Supreme Court's expectation (*Lego v. Twomey*, 1972), subjects viewed the negatively coerced confession as involuntary *and* they exhibited a relatively low rate of conviction (i.e., lower than in the no-constraint condition). However, when presented with testimony indicating that the defendant had confessed in response to a reward offer, subjects did not fully discount the confession. Under these circumstances, they decided that the confession was coerced but nevertheless used the evidence and voted guilty (i.e., compared to the no-constraint condition). In short, positively coerced confessions pose an evidentiary problem for the courts.

The primary question posed by this experiment was, can the often employed instruction effectively curb jurors' use of the positively coerced confession? As it turned out, the instruction manipulation had two interesting effects (or lack thereof). First, compared to the uninstructed subjects, those who had received the elaborated instruction generally conceded that more pressure to confess was exerted on the suspect. Yet the instruction did not affect the practically important variable—judgments of voluntariness. Second, and perhaps more disturbing, these instructions also had no influence on verdicts despite the finding that subjects *claimed* that it *had* influenced their guilty/not guilty decisions. This pattern thus reveals a fascinating discrepancy between the actual impact of the judge's charge and subjects' self-reported beliefs about that effect. On the positive side, it should be noted that although the judge's instruction did not achieve its full purpose, it also did not produce the boomerang effect reported by others (Broeder, 1959; Wolf & Montgomery, 1977).

Overall, it appears that an instruction by the judge does not mitigate the positive coercion bias. It is premature, however, to dismiss totally the potential utility of instructions, because they did affect certain dependent measures. Instead, it might be helpful to speculate about why they failed and to test how they could be improved.

Recall that there are two reasons why coerced confessions might be deemed inadmissible as evidence—(a) they are unconstitutional and unfair to the accused, and (b) they are unreliable and untrustworthy. A close look at the elaborated (long-form) instruction shows that it emphasizes the latter and neglects to advance the "fairness" justification. Yet Kalven and Zeisel (1966), citing real-world examples, suggested that "the jury may not so much consider the credibility of the confession as the impropriety of the method by which it was obtained" (p. 320). This observation implies that one promising approach to improving the elaborated instruction is to shift its emphasis—perhaps an argument that emphasizes what Kalven and Zeisel call the "sympathy hypothesis" rather than the "credibility hypothesis" might prove effective.

A fourth experiment (Kassin & Wrightsman, 1981) was conducted in order to (a) test the conceptual replicability of our results using a different stimulus trial, and (b) compose and test a "sympathy instruction," that is, one that makes salient the unconstitutionality and unfairness of any coerced confession. Specifically, subjects read a hypothetical assault case involving either an unconstrained or positively coerced confession, and received either no special instruction, the standard credibility instruction, a sympathy instruction, or one that encompasses both arguments. It was hypothesized that although the positive coercion bias would appear, it would be mitigated by the delivery of a sympathy instruction.

An 18-19 page adaptation of the Adams-Zemp assault case, originally created by Thibaut and Walker (1975), served as the stimulus trial. The transcript was written with the prescaled facts provided by Thibaut and Walker and presented as a criminal trial titled "*Adams v. Illinois.*" In this case, Samuel Adams is charged with assault for stabbing and seriously injuring Michael Zemp with a piece of broken glass during a heated argument in a tavern. The defense claimed that Adams, feeling threatened and endangered, had acted in self-defense. The entire transcript contained the examination of seven witnesses, including the defendant and the victim. Pretesting revealed that the no-confession version of the trial elicited a relatively low (22%) rate of conviction.

As in the third experiment, information about the confession and the circumstances surrounding it was introduced through the testimony of an arresting police officer to whom the defendant had allegedly confessed. In the confession evidence conditions (i.e., no-constraint, positive-constraint, and the negative-constraint control group), the officer testified that when he questioned Adams about the stabbing, the defendant confessed "that he had stabbed Michael Zemp without provocation." In the no-confession control group, the officer testified that in response to his inquiry, the defendant said "that he was afraid Mr. Zemp was about to attack him." The coercion manipulations were nearly identical to those of the first experiment. That is, Adams confessed either on his own initiative, in response to a threat, in response to an offer, or not at all.

The transcript concluded with one of four versions of the judge's instruction to the jury. Subjects in the no-instruction condition received a general charge that made no special reference to the confession issue. Subjects in the credibility instruction condition read the long-form instruction that was employed in Experiment 3—they were thus informed of the danger that an accused person might be persuaded to confess to acts he or she did not commit in an effort to avoid punishment or secure a reward (e.g., a suspended sentence). In the sympathy condition, the basic confession/voluntariness instruction was embellished as follows: ". . . because it is constitutionally unfair to an accused person who is under arrest for an officer of the law to pressure him through threats or trick him through offers of immunity into admitting to something against his will. Such tactics violate the individual's constitutional right to due process of law." A fourth instruction condition was included in which the credibility and sympathy arguments were combined.

After reading a version of the transcript, subjects completed a questionnaire individually and without deliberation. The major dependent measures from Experiment 3 were included: voluntariness judgments and verdicts were followed by reasonable doubt and probability-of-commission estimates. In addition, subjects were asked, in two separate questions, "how many out of 100 truly guilty (innocent) people do you think would have confessed to the arresting officer in this case?" This question was designed to assess lay beliefs about the normativeness of true and false confessions under the different instructions and constraint circumstances. Finally, all subjects rated, on a 9-point scale, how fairly the defendant was treated upon his arrest. This question was designed to assess subjects' attitudes along the sympathy dimension.

Verdicts

An overall significant difference between the four no-instruction groups corroborates the pattern of results repeatedly obtained for the Ron Oliver case in the earlier studies. That is, the conviction rate was highest in the confession-no constraint group (67%) and lowest in the no-confession group (10%). Moreover, whereas the negatively coerced confession (37%) did not significantly increase the proportion of guilty verdicts (i.e., compared to the no-confession group), the positively induced confession (56%) did have that damaging effect. A one-way analysis of variance on the combined verdict-confidence measure yielded a similarly significant difference—post hoc tests showed that these conviction scores were increased significantly only by the unconstrained and positively constrained confessions.

The conviction rates were 57% in the unconstrained confession condition and 51% in the positive inducement condition. It can also be seen that the instruction manipulation did not significantly affect verdicts. A two-way analysis of variance on the verdict-confidence measure similarly revealed no significant effects. In short, subjects were uniformly as likely to vote guilty for a defendant who confessed in response to a positive form of inducement as they were for one who confessed on his own accord.

Voluntariness Judgments

Whereas 100% of the subjects judged the unconstrained confession to be voluntary, only 67% found the positively induced confession to have been voluntarily given and only 53% decided as such for the negatively coerced confession.

Subjects clearly did distinguish between the unconstrained and positively constrained confessions (81% vs. 48% judged voluntary across types of instruction). Second, the type of instruction delivered by the judge affected the overall frequency of voluntariness judgments. Subsequent tests indicated a lower proportion of voluntariness decisions with the combined instruction (49%) than with no instruction (83%). Neither the sympathy nor credibility instruction *alone* (63% and 65%, respectively) significantly reduced the perception of voluntariness. An analysis of the voluntariness-confidence measure corroborated the above result. Main effects were obtained for constraint and type of instruction, the latter result again reflecting a significant difference between the no-instruction and combined instruction conditions. The interaction between constraint and instruction was not significant.

The major results of Experiment 4 may be recapitulated as follows:

1. The positive coercion bias was replicated. That is, even though subjects acknowledged that the positively constrained confession was relatively involuntary (and even though they asserted a relatively high standard of proof as necessary for conviction), they did not discount that evidence when rendering their verdicts.

2. The sympathy appeal, present in the sympathy and combined instruction conditions, significantly increased subjects' perception that the defendant was unfairly treated. Of the four levels of instruction, however, only the combined condition was even partially effective—it successfully lowered the frequency of voluntary judgments but it failed to lower the conviction rate.

It was noted in Chapter 2 that conceptions of coercion have essentially progressed through three stages—(a) negative/physical pressure, (b) negative/physical or psychological pressure, and (c) positive or negative/physical or psychological pressure. Within this historical guideline, the present program of research suggests that the lay person, the potential juror, is, in a sense, fixated at the second stage. Subjects readily acknowledged that a mere threat, even without signs of physical brutality, is coercive enough to elicit an unreliable confession. Yet they seem unable or unwilling to excuse a defendant whose admission is induced by the promise of immunity or reward— this despite the recognition that accused persons might plausibly confess to acts they did not commit. The basis for this anomaly is clarified somewhat by subjects' response to the strength-of-pressure question in Experiment 3, which showed that despite their assumed equivalence, subjects viewed the promise of reward as simply a weaker form of inducement than a threat of punishment.

Judicial Instruction

Experiments 3 and 4 were designed primarily to assess the utility of judicial instruction as a mechanism for reducing the positive coercion bias. As it turned out, our results on this issue are mixed. Experiment 3 demonstrated quite clearly that the currently available forms of the instruction are ineffective. Instruction effects were obtained on certain dependent variables, but not on the two practically important judgments. Experiment 4 revealed that although no instruction significantly affected verdicts, the dual instruction (i.e., emphasizing both the unfairness and the unreliability of an induced confession) did significantly alter subjects' voluntariness judgments. The potential importance of this latter result should not be overlooked. After all, in numerous state courts, jurors are explicitly instructed to consider/ignore a confession in their verdicts on the basis of their decisions about voluntariness. Indeed these results suggest that the two decisions were highly interrelated. Across all confession groups, the correlation between voluntariness-confidence scores and verdict-confidence scores was .55 in Experiment 3 and .48 in Experiment 4.

According to police and court statistics, pretrial confessions—both disputed and undisputed—are prevalent in criminal cases (Kalven & Zeisel, 1966; Zimbardo, 1967). For years, legal scholars and philosophers have debated about the *actual* probative value of voluntary and involuntary confessions. The present research suggests that it is equally important to investigate jurors' *beliefs* about their probative value.

From a practical standpoint, the results of Experiments 3 and 4 are discouraging because they collectively suggest that positively coerced confessions are a problem and that judicial instruction might not be an effective solution. Still, another issue should be addressed before drawing any firm negative conclusions. Can the timing of the confession-voluntariness instruction mediate its impact? In the present research, the judge's instruction followed the presentation of evidence, as is common practice in most courts. Yet two studies have shown that certain types of judicial instruction affect mock jurors' decisions only when they *precede* the evidence (Elwork, Sales, & Alfini, 1977; Kassin & Wrightsman, 1979). Perhaps this finding holds for the confession instruction. It is thus possible that subjects had tentatively decided on their *verdicts* before the instruction was delivered and so were subsequently influenced only in their *voluntariness* judgments. Experiment 5, which we did in collaboration with Teddy Warner, looked at this possibility (Kassin & Wrightsman, 1985).

A second important question that remains is, does the positive coercion bias persist or disappear after a jury deliberates and, if it persists, is judicial instruction any more effective a device at this group level? Our earlier research had focused on the beliefs and judgments of the individual, nondeliberating juror.

To investigate these possibilities, Experiment 5 had 102 five- and six-person juries read a version of the assault case, and receive the combined (credibility and fairness) or standard (i.e., no mention of voluntariness) instruction either before or after the presentation of evidence. The groups were then given 30 minutes to deliberate and arrive at a unanimous verdict. As it turned out, the conviction rate was somewhat lower in the positively constrained than unconstrained confession conditions (27% and 43%, respectively), but this difference was not statistically significant. When broken down by instruction condition, we found that although this pattern held for the uninstructed (41% and 49%), there was a significant difference among those groups that received the special charge (13% and 40%). In short, positively coerced confessions were rejected by juries who received the double-barreled voluntariness instruction.

Experiment 6 in this line of research (Kassin & McNall, 1991) took a somewhat different approach, by focusing on techniques in which the police interrogator either exaggerates the strength of the evidence and the magnitude of the charges—called maximization—

or the interrogator mitigates the crime and plays down the seriousness of the offense—called minimization (see Chapter 4). Does this
variation affect mock jurors' reactions to a confession resulting from
the interrogation?

In Experiment 6, 75 subjects participated as mock jurors in exchange for money or course credit. Subjects were randomly assigned
either to a no-confession control group or to one of four conditions
receiving confession evidence: unprompted, a promise of leniency,
a threat of punishment, or minimization. The Ron Oliver trial transcript was used once more.

All five versions of the transcript were identical except for a
variation in confession evidence. In the control group with no confession, the arresting officer testified that the defendant had flatly
denied having stolen the car. In the remaining four groups, the same
officer testified that Ron Oliver confessed upon arrest. In each of
these conditions, a sentence in the prosecutor's closing argument was
also varied to reflect the circumstances of the confession. In the
promise and *threat* conditions, the inducements to confess were like
those used in previous experiments.

In the *minimization* condition, which was added in Experiment 6,
the police officer elicited Oliver's confession by saying "that I didn't
think taking the car was such a terrible thing, that there was probably
a misunderstanding, and that I really didn't find his actions that unusual" followed by "it's easy to see how a person could be tempted into
taking the car. I mean, here's this dealership with hundreds of cars on
the lot, if I didn't already have a car, and probably couldn't afford one,
there's no telling what I'd do, either. Besides, I told him, just as I can
see how he might have been tempted in the first place, I can also
understand how hard it would be to return the car once it's too late."

Finally, in the *unprompted* confession group, as in previous vol-
untary-confession treatments, the officer recounted his conversation
with Oliver, and claimed that the defendant admitted on his own
initiative that he stole the car.

Out of the 60 subjects in Experiment 6 who read transcripts
containing a confession, 23 (38%) considered it voluntary. Signifi-

cant between-group differences indicated that subjects who read about an unprompted confession were more likely to judge it as voluntary (93% did) than those in the promise condition (with 20%), threat condition (13%), or minimization condition (27%).

A more sensitive measure of opinions on the voluntariness—the combining of the judgments and confidence ratings—revealed significant differences that closely paralleled the dichotomous judgment data. Indeed, the same pattern appeared in ratings of how much pressure the arresting officer had placed on the defendant, as subjects in the control and unprompted confession groups perceived greater pressure than those in the remaining conditions. The results are clear: subjects perceived the confession as involuntary *whenever* it was prompted by statements made by the interrogator.

With regard to verdicts in Experiment 6, overall, 32 subjects voted guilty, and 43 voted not guilty, for a 43% rate of conviction. An inspection of the verdicts in the five conditions revealed dramatic differences, as the conviction rates were 6% for the no-confession control group, 60% with an unprompted confession, 53% under promise, 27% under threat, and 67% under minimization.

The measure that combined verdicts and confidence levels produced results that paralleled the verdict measure. Post hoc comparisons indicated that the conviction rate was not affected by confessions made in response to an explicit threat. Yet convictions were more frequent when the defendant confessed following a promise of leniency, and then increased again when he confessed without prompting or in response to minimization.

These results are informative in a number of respects. First, as indicated by the very low conviction rate of 6% in the control group, the case against the defendant was extremely weak. Second, the addition of the unprompted confession had a powerful impact, increasing the conviction rate to 60%. Third, as found in the earlier experiments, subjects were not significantly moved by those confessions that were elicited by a threat of punishment (27%). Fourth, the conviction rate increased markedly when the defendant confessed in response to either a promise of leniency (53%) or minimization remarks (67%).

SUMMARY AND CONCLUSIONS

Our research has shown that despite the courts' modern treatment of promises and threats as equivalent conditions of coercion, jurors react very differently to these two circumstances. When a suspect was said to have confessed in response to a threat of harm or punishment, even without signs of physical brutality, mock jurors fully rejected that evidence. When the inducement took the form of a promise of leniency, however, subjects were unable or unwilling to excuse the defendant completely and discount his confession. Under these circumstances, they tended to vote for conviction despite having conceded that the confession was, by law, involuntary. On the individual juror level, this phenomenon has proven to be quite robust and resistant to the effects of judicial instruction, even that which explicitly cites positive forms of constraint as coercive and potentially unreliable. On the encouraging side, recent research has shown that our own instruction, written to articulate both the credibility and fairness rationales, did eliminate the positive coercion bias among deliberating mock juries.

Our research represents a modest first step in our understanding of how juries view confession evidence in all its complexity. As such, several important questions remain unresolved. For example, why did mock jurors react so differently to the two types of constraint? Part of the answer is simply that people view the promise of reward as a weaker form of behavioral inducement than a threat of punishment. Our own data provided mixed support for this hypothesis. In one study, we had subjects rate the degree of pressure exerted on the defendant to confess and found that these ratings were significantly higher in the negative- than positive-constraint situation. In the same study, however, we asked subjects to estimate the percentages of guilty and innocent people who would confess under the circumstances of the case they had read, and found that the promise and threat conditions were virtually identical on this measure. Parenthetically, it is interesting to note that across constraint conditions, subjects estimated that 46% of truly guilty people and 36% of truly innocent people would confess. The latter figure is especially surprising, because it suggests that people do clearly recognize the risk of false confession.

SEVEN

The Psychologist as Expert Witness

Chapters 5 and 6 indicate that relevant psychological theory and persuasive psychological research provide a resounding "No" to the question: Do jurors fully understand the nature and determinants of confessions introduced as part of the prosecution evidence in a criminal trial? But psychologists have *very* rarely testified in trials as experts witnesses regarding confession evidence.

EARLY EFFORTS TO TESTIFY

This absence exists despite a long history of willingness to testify. As noted in Chapter 5, Hugo Münsterberg (1908), who founded the psychological laboratory at Harvard University in 1892, became involved in two highly publicized cases around the turn of the century. In 1906 a Chicago woman was raped and murdered; Richard Ivens discovered the body and immediately reported it to the police. Looking tired and disheveled, he became a suspect and was interrogated by the police. Although he initially denied the allegations, he later—according to the police—confessed repeatedly, enriching his story on each successive occasion (Münsterberg, 1908). At the trial, the district attorney based his case on the confession evidence. Professor Münsterberg concluded that Ivens's confession might have been a result of hypnotic induction, and offered to testify, but he was not allowed to. Even though Ivens repudiated his statements to the police and produced 16 unimpeached witnesses to substantiate his alibi, he was convicted and later executed.

Münsterberg's other effort to apply psychological knowledge to assessment of the credibility of a confession brought less acclaim to this approach. In 1907, "Big Bill" Haywood, the leader of the IWW (International Workers of the World) was charged with conspiracy to murder Frank Steunenberg, a former governor of Idaho and a well-known opponent to organized labor. On December 30, 1905, in Caldwell, ID, Steunenberg had opened the gate to his modest home and was blown apart by a waiting bomb. The murder trial transformed Haywood into an international symbol of labor protest; Clarence Darrow offered his services as defense attorney, and people like Eugene V. Debs and Maxim Gorky rallied support (Hale, 1980; Holbrook, 1957).

The case against Haywood rested on the testimony of Harry Orchard, a one-time IWW organizer who—after a 4-day interrogation—confessed to committing the bombing (as well as many other crimes) at the behest of an "inner circle" of radicals, including Haywood. Münsterberg examined Orchard in his cell, during Haywood's trial, and conducted 100 tests on him over a period of 7 hours; in Münsterberg's mind, the most important of these was the word association test. Upon returning to Cambridge, Münsterberg permitted an interview with the *Boston Herald,* which quoted him as saying, "Orchard's confession is every word of it true" (Hale, 1980, p. 117). This disclosure, coming before a verdict had been delivered, threatened the impartiality of the trial. Still, the jury found Haywood not guilty, as the state did not produce any significant evidence corroborating Orchard's confession, as Idaho required. Two weeks later, Münsterberg slightly amended his position by introducing the concept of "subjective truthfulness." His free association tests, he now concluded, revealed that Orchard genuinely believed he was telling the truth, but they couldn't discern the actual facts of the matter.

Perhaps one reason for the limited number of more recent examples of psychologists testifying on such issues was the fact that Münsterberg maintained his exaggerated claims for his science. In a letter to the editor he wrote: "To deny that the experimental psychol-

ogist has indeed possibilities of determining the 'truth-telling' process is just as absurd as to deny that the chemical expert can find out
whether there is arsenic in a stomach or whether blood spots are of
human or animal origin" (quoted by Hale, 1980, p. 118). His claims
took on exaggerated metaphors; he could "pierce into the mind" and
bring to light its deepest secrets.

STANDARDS FOR ADMISSIBILITY

Münsterberg, despite his exaggerations, was correct in emphasizing that psychology had evidence that the judge and jury couldn't intuit
(Wells, 1984). The breadth in testimony by psychologists currently
allowed is impressive; Nietzel and Dillehay (1986) list the following as
only some of the topics for which expert psychological opinion is
solicited: Competence to stand trial, insanity defense, civil commitment, child custody, guardianship and conservatorship, and adoption.

Perhaps the topic that has generated the greatest amount of recent
discussion is the appropriateness of psychologists' testifying as expert witnesses on the accuracy of eyewitness identification. Fulero
(1988) concluded that psychologists have been allowed to testify
about eyewitness accuracy for the defense in at least 450 cases in 25
states, but many states still prevent them from doing so.

Furthermore, a survey by Kassin, Ellsworth, and Smith (1989) of
63 experts on eyewitness testimony reported that at least 80% of
these psychologists agreed that research results on this issue were
consistent enough to present in court; the specific aspects of eyewitness accuracy that were surveyed included the relationship between
accuracy and confidence, the lineup instructions, the impact of
exposure time, and unconscious transference. More than 70% of
experts believed that the tendency to overestimate the duration of an
event, the cross-racial identification bias of white witnesses, and
lineup fairness generated consistent research findings. In addition,
leading researchers (Buckhout, 1986; Loftus, 1983; Wells, 1986)
agree with the above, and they have repeatedly testified when asked.

Given this breadth of types of testimony, what qualifies a person
for acceptance as an expert? Typically, the courts have allowed an

expert to testify if the intent of the expert's testimony has general acceptance among the scientific community of the particular field to which it belongs. This standard is called the Frye criterion (from *Frye v. United States,* 1923). But other courts have applied a less stringent standard, based on their interpretation of a rule of evidence adopted for the federal courts by Congress in 1975. This rule, Rule 702 in the revised Federal Rules of Evidence, basically allows experts who are qualified in their fields to present their conclusions to a jury, "even if those conclusions are idiosyncratic or outside the consensus in the field, if the testimony is relevant to the case and will help the jury 'to understand the evidence or to determine a fact' " (Greenhouse, 1992, p. A9). The U.S. Supreme Court announced that it would, during its 1992-1993 term, decide between these standards.

How much should judges play the role of gatekeepers, screening out what they consider to be undesirable testimony? Or should juries be permitted to have the testimony of experts to assist them in their role of fact finders? In two recent cases, psychologists were utilized to present their perspective on the facts. In each of these cases, at issue was the possibility that a defendant had confessed to a crime that he did not commit. His confession was admitted as part of the evidence by the prosecution.

Was it truly voluntary, or was it, to use the terminology introduced in Chapter 5, either coerced-compliant (in which the suspect has confessed only to escape the interrogation, gain a promised benefit, or avoid a threatened punishment) or—even more extreme—coerced-internalized (in which an innocent suspect confesses and comes to believe that he or she is guilty). We imagine that jurors don't give much credence to this third possibility, but these cases suggest that coerced-internalized confessions do occur.

THE PAUL INGRAM CASE: AN EXAMPLE OF
A COERCED-INTERNALIZED CONFESSION

In the state of Washington, Paul Ingram—a deeply religious man and a deputy sheriff and a county Republican Committee chair—was charged with incredibly heinous crimes: sexual abuse, the rape of his daughters, and Satanic cult crimes that included the slaughter of some 25 babies.

Over a period of 5 months in 1988, Ingram was interrogated 23 times by the police. He was kept in jail during this period. He was hypnotized, given graphic crime details, told by a psychologist that sex offenders often repress their offenses, and urged by a minister of his church to confess. The psychologist used a relaxation procedure with Ingram, as a result of which the suspect showed a heightened suggestibility. Leading questions by the police and the psychologist caused Ingram—who previously had reported no memory of the crimes—to visualize images of scenes involving group rapes and Satanic cult activities.

Eventually, Ingram did confess. He then "recalled" the crime scenes to specification and pleaded guilty. His pseudo-memories led him to be accused of scores of other crimes. For a time he came to believe the accuracy of these.

Paul Ingram is now serving 20 years in prison. Yet there is no physical evidence that any of the crimes occurred.

An expert social scientist played a unique role in this case. Richard Ofshe (1992) is a social psychologist and a professor of sociology at the University of California at Berkeley. Even though he was called as a witness by the state, he concluded that Ingram had been "brainwashed" into thinking he was a part of a Satanic cult. Sure enough, although Ingram initially said he could not recall the incident, he later confessed, and even embellished the story (Ofshe, 1992). In fact, Richard Ofshe, using similar procedures to those described above, was able to persuade Ingram that he committed other acts that never had occurred.

THE BRADLEY PAGE CASE: AN EXAMPLE OF
A COERCED-COMPLIANT CONFESSION

Whereas Paul Ingram's response to his interrogation is an example of a coerced-internalized confession, Bradley Page's reflects a type of coerced-compliant one. But both appear to us to be similar miscarriages of justice. (We know the specifics of Bradley Page's case because Elliot Aronson, a social psychologist, testified as a expert witness in the trial; we have relied on his accounts of this case; Aronson, 1990; Pratkanis & Aronson, 1991).

In the fall of 1987, Bradley Page and his fiancée, Bibi Lee—both students at the University of California, Berkeley—decided to go jogging in a heavily wooded park several miles from the campus. Their friend Robin accompanied them; the three of them drove to the park in Bradley Page's old station wagon.

After a few miles, Brad and Robin lost sight of Bibi—she was not as strong a runner. They stopped for her to catch up, but she didn't. Concerned, they retraced their path, with no results. They concluded that probably Bibi had wandered off the main trail, and so they returned to the parking lot, where they had left Brad's car, in the expectation that Bibi would meet them there at the previously agreed-upon time. After waiting 15 or 20 minutes or so, Brad decided that he should drive around the park by car, looking for Bibi, while Robin waited in the parking lot. He did so for about 15 minutes, and then returned, telling Robin he had been unable to find Bibi. Note that this was the only length of time that Brad was separated from Robin. The two waited in the parking lot a while longer, but Brad then told Robin he had to drive back to campus, as he had promised to take a group of his housemates to a museum. He said that Bibi could get back to campus easily by bus; he also suspected that she might have disappeared deliberately because the two of them had had a lovers' spat earlier that day and she had been annoyed at him; perhaps she was punishing him. (Once before when they had had a big fight, she had "disappeared" for a couple of days.)

That evening (Sunday night) he tried to call Bibi (who lived in another campus building) but was told she had not returned. At midnight she still had not surfaced. A search ensued; her disappearance was highly publicized in the San Francisco Bay area newspapers. Several witnesses came forward; one was a woman who reported that while driving home from church, she saw a burly, bearded man pulling and tugging a young woman (who fit Bibi's description) into a van; at the time she didn't know whether this was a playful or a violent act, so she didn't report it to the police until the newspapers publicized Bibi's disappearance.

Exactly 5 weeks after her disappearance, Bibi's body was found in a partial grave in a heavily wooded area of the park. It was concluded that the murderer—or someone—had had sexual intercourse with her dead body. Despite the fact that a serial rapist and killer in the area fit the witness's description of a burly, bearded man (and Brad Page did not), Brad Page became a police suspect. They hypothesized that during the 15 minutes that he was away from Robin, supposedly searching for Bibi in his car, he might have found her and killed her.

The procedures used by the police interrogators are worthy of special note, given the fact that most jurors assume that confessions are freely voluntary and hence truthful. First, the police established a friendly relationship with Brad Page; second, they lied to him about other evidence.

Twelve hours after he learned of Bibi Lee's death, Brad Page was brought in for questioning. The sense of false compatibility was established early. (These two detectives had questioned Page earlier, when Bibi Lee first disappeared.) The police read Page his *Miranda* rights but convinced him to waive the right to an attorney during the interrogation. "We're all friends here, aren't we?" they said. They befriended him, put their arm around him, and called him "son." But they asked Brad Page to go over his story again and again.

During the questioning, they kept asking him how he could possibly have left his fiancée alone in the woods and then driven back home. Page did feel guilty about it, saying several times, "It was the biggest mistake of my life!" Each time, he felt even more guilty.

Misrepresentations of the facts by the police interrogators took the following forms: First, they told Page that late on the night of the disappearance, he had been seen near the site of the shallow grave and that his fingerprints had been found on a rock that had been employed as the murder weapon. Also, they told him that he had failed the lie detector test he had agreed to take—another misrepresentation of the truth. As one of the detectives clasped his arm, they told him, "You better come clean. If you don't, your soul will rot. We're your friends; we urge you to come clean." (As noted in Chapters 3 and 4, overstatement or falsification of evidence as an *interrogation procedure* is permitted in most states.)

Bradley Page said that he was not aware that he had left his apartment that night and certainly had no idea how his fingerprints had gotten on the murder weapon, whatever it was. He was dumbfounded. "Someone saw me?" he asked.

But he had come to trust the interrogators as his friends, and, now terribly confused, asked them if it was possible for a person to commit a terrible crime like this and subsequently "blank it out." The interrogators said yes, such things were common occurrences! "It happens all the time; we want to help you get it out," they said.

At this point, accounts of what happened next, during the prolonged 9-hour interrogation, diverge. The police had taped the entire interrogation; in fact, Elliot Aronson, as an expert witness, had access to the audiotapes. But the police, inexplicably, had turned off the tape recorder for about 30 to 40 minutes during this crucial part of the questioning.

According to Page, the police told him "it might help him relieve his *guilty* conscience if he closed his eyes and tried to imagine how he *might* have killed Bibi *if he had killed her"* (Pratkanis & Aronson, 1991, p. 176). Brad Page did as (he claimed) he was told, constructing a detailed description of an assault on Bibi Lee, what he later described, at his trials, as an imaginative scenario. The police even persuaded him to speculate about the act of necrophilia. He later said that he came up with the scenario "and they kept correcting me." When told later that the police considered this an actual confession, he seemed genuinely astonished and immediately denied it. He refused to sign the typed confession they placed before him. (The police dispute that they asked this hypothetical question; they say that they asked Page straightforwardly how he committed the crime.)

Page was surprised that the police concluded that he had really confessed; he felt they were his friends, who might—under other circumstances—invite him home to dinner.

Robin testified at the first trial that there was some tension between the two on the way to the park. This evidence—limited as it was—fit with the police speculation that Page had murdered his fiancée out of anger toward her. Even though a great many details of this disputed confession were inconsistent with the actual physical evidence, Brad Page was indicted for first-degree murder, implying a planned, premeditated killing of another. In his first trial, the jury was unable to agree on a unanimous verdict, although the 8 of the 12 jurors voted for a conviction.

Prior to the second trial, the court-appointed defense attorney contacted Elliot Aronson, because as a social psychologist, Aronson was an expert on persuasion. He listened to the tapes of the interrogation 20 times or more, and observed how the confession was very tentative whereas everything else Bradley Page said was very authoritative and straightforward. Aronson concluded that the confession was not valid. For apparently the first time a social psychologist was allowed to testify about social influence and coercion in the interrogation room. But the judge restricted Aronson's testimony to scientific studies and findings—for example, on obedience and the Asch conformity studies—and ruled that he couldn't render an opinion whether Page was tricked by the police into a false confession, thus diminishing the effect of the expert witness's testimony. Aronson did testify that most people will believe false information from people they trust.

In this second trial, the jury was also in disagreement for an extended time, but after deliberating for 6 days, the jury unanimously found Bradley Page not guilty of murder, but guilty of voluntary manslaughter. He was sentenced to 9 years in prison. His appeal is currently under review for two reasons, one being that the psychologist-expert was not allowed to testify about the nature of Page's confession.

WHAT DOES PSYCHOLOGICAL TESTIMONY HAVE TO OFFER?

Before dealing with specific contributions that can be made by the psychologist as an expert witness, we need to consider the role of the expert. Münsterberg, 100 years ago, did not hesitate to take sides; he played the role of an advocate. Elizabeth Loftus, who frequently testifies in criminal trials for the defense, puts it this way:

> Should a psychologist in a court of law act as an advocate for the defense or an impartial educator? My answer to that question, if I

am completely honest, is *both*. If I believe in his innocence with
all my heart and soul, then I probably can't help but become an
advocate of sorts. (Loftus & Ketcham, 1991, p. 238)

In contrast, when preparing to testify in the Bradley Page trial, Elliot
Aronson scrupulously refused to meet Bradley Page, and when asked
by Page's attorney if he thought Page was guilty, Aronson responded,
"I don't know." His purpose was to testify about the effect of the
interrogation techniques on the likelihood of a false confession,
which is a separate issue from the guilt of the defendant. As Brigham
notes, "Loftus' implication that one will become an advocate could
prove destructive in the creative hands of an aggressive attorney who
is seeking to destroy an impartial expert witness's credibility" (1992,
p. 529). Furthermore, in the survey by Kassin et al. (1989), the
experts said that they were as willing to testify for the prosecution
as for the defense.

   In general, what psychologists have to offer is, in Aronson's
words, "making sense of a senseless situation." They can describe
how conditions can increase the risk of a false confession, how being
suspected, or generalized feelings of guilt, can create a susceptibility
to being influenced by skilled interrogators. They can bring psychological concepts to bear upon the distinction between voluntary and
coerced confessions, and help jurors make connections between
situational influences and behavior. They can illustrate how we make
attributions based on personal dispositions and often commit the
fundamental attribution error. As the research findings of Chapter 6
implied, jurors may ignore such admonitions, but some may benefit
from the information. In that sense, psychologists as expert witnesses
can be advocates for truth while being impartial educators.

EIGHT

The Future of Confessions

The goal of this book has been to provide a comprehensive review of the place of criminal confessions, including an examination of their place in the development of our legal system and their impact upon the verdicts of modern-day jurors. This is a critical time to reassess the role of confession evidence because of the recent *Fulminante* decision. What does the future hold?

Confessions have been a recurring source of controversy. Will they continue to be so? The purpose of this chapter is to offer our views on several trends and needs.

AN INCREASE IN DISPUTED CONFESSIONS

As noted in Chapter 3, in 1991 the U.S. Supreme Court in *Arizona v. Fulminante* heard an appeal by a defendant, Oreste Fulminante, who had been convicted of murder on the basis of a confession. Prior to his arrest on this charge, but after the murder had occurred, Fulminante was in prison, where he was befriended by a fellow inmate who was actually a paid informant for the FBI masquerading as an organized crime figure. The informant told Fulminante that he would be subject to rough treatment from other inmates because of the rumor that he had murdered a child, and the informant offered him protection in exchange for a confession. Only then did Fulminante confess to the murder. There was no other evidence, but on the basis of the confession—which Fulminante later claimed was coerced—he was convicted and sentenced to death.

On appeal, the Arizona Supreme Court ruled (a) that the confession was coerced because Fulminante feared for his safety without protection; and (b) that its admission was prejudicial error. Thus the court reversed the conviction and ordered that a new trial be held without the confession. Given this outcome, the state chose to appeal to the U.S. Supreme Court. The court decided to rule on this issue and made a surprising and unprecedented decision. In recent years the Supreme Court has broadened its view of what constitutes a voluntary statement, and has approved confessions that formerly were ruled inadmissible. In this case, the Supreme Court went an important step further. It conceded that Fulminante's confession was coerced and that its admission at trial was prejudicial error—because there was no corroborating evidence. But by a 5-to-4 margin, the Court also concluded that, in general, erroneously admitted confessions are subject to the so-called harmless error rule; that is, if there is other evidence sufficient to convict the defendant without a confession and if an inadmissible (i.e., coerced) confession sneaks into the evidence, no harm has resulted from its inclusion.

The decision was astounding. Ever since 1897 in federal trials and 1936 in state trials, the assumption has been that forcing suspects to incriminate themselves, through coercion (physical abuse, threats, or promises of leniency) was such deplorable conduct that the use of its results made a fair trial impossible ("The Supreme Court's Harmful Error," 1991). It was automatic that the presence of coerced confession evidence in the trial justified a retrial.

The five justices who voted in the majority on the section of the decision that concluded that the "harmless error" doctrine could apply included four who had been appointed by Presidents Reagan and Bush, plus William Rehnquist, who was elevated to the position of Chief Justice by President Reagan. When their decision was announced in March 1991, supporters of the rights of suspects and defendants were outraged. *The New York Times,* in an editorial, stated: "The injection of the harmless error notion was a wild extension of the otherwise valid principle that minor technical mistakes, which inevitably creep into most cases, should not invalidate a fundamentally fair trial, especially if the independent evidence of guilt is overwhelming" ("The Supreme Court's Harmful Error," 1991, p. A12). Columnist Anthony Lewis (1991) observed that the decision "simply ignored decades of decisions holding that a conviction based even in part on a coerced confession [in the words of Justice Felix Frankfurter] 'cannot stand' " (1991, p. A15).

What would be the impact of the *Fulminante* decision? Would it lead to an increase in police pressures in more coerced confessions? The initial reaction by experts was mixed. Professor Paul Rothstein of the Georgetown University Law Center, quoted in the *National Law Journal* (Coyle & Lavelle, 1991), predicted that it would affect relatively few cases. "In cases of blatant coercion, prosecutors wouldn't introduce it and a judge wouldn't let it in," he was quoted as saying (Coyle & Lavelle, 1991, p. 27).

Others were less sanguine. *The New York Times* editorial predicted that: "Instead of steering clear of questionable confessions, police, prosecutors and trial judges are now invited to search for rationales for obtaining and using them in the hope that judges will manage to find the trial fair anyway" ("The Supreme Court's Harmful Error," 1991, p. A12). Likewise, *Time* magazine quoted legal experts who feared that in borderline cases—ones that prosecutors previously would not have brought to trial—the temptation will be to introduce questionable confessions in the hope that any resulting conviction will be upheld on appeal (Lacayo, 1991).

Which view reflects the circumstances in the time since the *Fulminante* decision? It is too early to have any objective data, but our strong impression is that a greater number of disputed confessions are coming forward. When we talk to defense attorneys, they tell us they have more clients than before who claim that they have been coerced by the police into a confession. Judges are more willing to allow these dubious confessions into evidence. Our feeling is that, unless something intervenes, the *Fulminante* decision will reverse the pattern of the past 70 years, in which the courts have sought to protect us against violations of due process and to minimize the risk that innocent people confess to crimes they did not commit.

SOURCES OF CHANGE

If our interpretation of recent developments is correct, and a greater number of coerced (and false) confessions are being induced, what are the possible remedies?

Throughout the 200 years of federal government, the legislative branch has served as a corrective agent against what were considered extreme actions by the courts. Sometimes, in the view of the Congress, the Court has become too liberal; for example, after the *Miranda* decision and other decisions by the Warren Court favoring defendant's rights, the U.S. Congress sought legislative relief against these decisions.

Six months after the *Fulminante* decision was announced, the Judiciary Committee of the U.S. House of Representatives voted to negate that decision. A section was inserted into the 1991 crime control bill to add a provision to the federal laws that no coerced confession could be considered a harmless error. The bill did not become adopted as a law, but we anticipate that the change in the constituency of Congress in 1993 will produce further legislative efforts in this direction.

"MORE RESEARCH IS NEEDED"

A theme of this book is the paucity of social science research on reactions to confession evidence. To paraphrase the closing statement of many journal articles, further research is needed.

Voluntariness and coercion remain ambiguous terms, both for the courts and the public. Box 8.1 presents one effort to clarify their meaning.

Can Jurors Disregard a Confession?

Our research leads to the conclusion that juries are heavily influenced by the presence of a confession as a part of the prosecutor's evidence. But on occasion a jury disregards a confession—even a voluntary

BOX 8.1
A Dimension of Voluntariness Versus Involuntariness

Can people agree as to what is a voluntary confession? Are there differences in the perceptions of confessions under different circumstances? We asked 79 college students to react to 41 different confessions, each given under different circumstances. The subjects' task was to rate how voluntary or involuntary each confession was, on a 7-point scale (7 = completely voluntary, 1 = completely involuntary). The mean ratings for some "benchmark" confessions are given below.

Mean Ratings

1. A suspect breaks a law he thinks is immoral; suspect immediately turns himself in. 6.31
2. Suspect comes to the police station and turns himself in for a crime for which he wasn't even a suspect. 6.35
3. Suspect is put in a cell and left there. He is fed at appropriate times, has bathroom facilities, and is questioned only briefly each day. After being detained for 10 days, he confesses. 4.23
4. Confesses only after he is promised a lenient sentence if he confesses. 3.41
5. Suspect is questioned for 6 hours at which point he asks for a bathroom break. He is denied, and then he confesses. 2.79
6. Suspect confesses only after he is threatened with severe punishment if he fails to confess and is still convicted. 2.39
7. A man is placed in solitary confinement, in an unlighted cell and given only bread and water. After one month he confesses. 1.80
8. Suspect is beaten, tortured, kept several days without food. Only then does he confess. 1.80
9. Suspect is questioned, then given 10 very severe electric shocks over a 15-minute period. Only after these shocks does he confess. 1.55

confession—and finds the defendant not guilty. The trial of Bernhard Goetz, the "subway vigilante," is illustrative, and raises the research question: Under what circumstances is a confession disregarded?

Just 3 days before Christmas of 1984, four young men were shot by a gunman as they were riding a New York City subway. Nine days later, Bernhard Goetz, a 37-year-old electronics expert, surrendered to police in Concord, New Hampshire. The confession, which he repeated a few hours later in the presence of New York City police and prosecutors, was as voluntary as one could imagine. Although Goetz was, by then, one of the many suspects in the case, his whereabouts were unknown to the New York City police when he spontaneously surfaced and appeared at the Concord police station.

Goetz was later brought to trial on charges of attempted murder, reckless endangerment, and illegal gun possession, and the entire nation followed his case with intense interest. Sentiment in New York City—and across the country—was divided over whether Goetz was an armed racist intent on harm or a potential robbery victim who acted in self-defense. His confession, which was videotaped and shown to the jury, seemed to be among the most damaging evidence. He even told the police that after firing once at each of the four young men he noticed that one of them did not seem to be as wounded as the others. He later claimed that he walked over to that youth and said, "You seem to be doing all right; here's another," firing another bullet into the young man's body. (This description was a matter of controversy at the trial, however.)

But Barry Slotnik, Goetz's defense attorney, was able to cast doubt on the accuracy of such details in his own client's confession. Other evidence, such as the observations by other passengers on the subway car, didn't jibe with Goetz's report that he paused between the fourth and fifth shots. Testimony by a medical expert questioned whether it was possible for the young man to have been sitting as he was so described by Goetz (Fletcher, 1988).

In essence, the jury, during its deliberations, came to accept the defense team's portrayal of the events. In keeping with his attorney's suggestion, they concluded that Goetz's confession contained false recollections—false because of the rage that set in after the event, plus his being distraught and confused after being on the run for 9 days (Fletcher, 1988). One juror told a reporter, "It happened rapidly. I didn't think he had time to think" (Press, 1987, p. 21). Another said: "He was so agitated. . . . He just wasn't being natural" (Friedrich,

1987, p. 11). Goetz was found not guilty of all the charges except one minor one, that he possessed a gun illegally.

Do the results of the Goetz trial generalize to other cases? Only under special circumstances. The fear of subway crime in New York City (4 of the 12 jurors were previous victims of subway muggings) doubtless provided a context for the jurors' reactions to the confession. But this case study tells us that in those trials in which there is physical evidence that conflicts with statements in the confession *and* a talented attorney to exploit it, the jury might disregard the confession.

Effects of Interrogation Procedures

In addition to the empirical questions we have gleaned from the laws of confession evidence and procedure, innumerable others of conceptual interest to psychologists and of practical value to the judiciary await experimentation. For example, Chapter 4 observes that in recent years law-enforcement officials have begun videotaping interrogation sessions for presentation in court. As such, the jury is enabled to view the confession and its surrounding circumstances directly rather than through the testimony of a witness. How does this procedural innovation affect jurors' perceptions of voluntariness and the inferences they draw from confession evidence? Based on the fact that people tend to attribute causality to that which is perceptually salient (see Taylor & Fiske, 1978), Lassiter and Irvine (1986) tested the hypothesis that judgments of voluntariness in videotaped confessions would be systematically biased by the camera angle. A mock interrogation resulting in a confession was thus videotaped from three angles so that either the interrogators, the suspect, or both were visually salient. Subjects watched one of these versions of the episode. Sure enough, their judgments of coercion were lowest when the suspect was salient, highest when the interrogator was salient, and intermediate when the two were equally visible. In short, this seemingly trivial detail of procedure can, as attribution psychologists would predict, have a marked effect on juries' perceptions of confession evidence.

Our research has demonstrated the possible dangers inherent in so-called subtle methods of interrogation, similar to those described in Chapter 4. Minimization, a technique in which the interrogator lulls the suspect into a false sense of security by mitigating the crime, making excuses for the suspect, or blaming the victim, may seem to be noncoercive; yet it may communicate an implicit offer of leniency (i.e., a relatively light sentence for the suspect who does confess).

The functional equivalence of minimization and a subtle promise of lenient treatment can be argued on two grounds. First, the police use of minimization and maximization have the potential to coax innocent people into confessing to crimes they didn't commit. How often this actually occurs is impossible to estimate. The question needs to be examined under laboratory conditions in which precise estimates can be determined. What would be appropriate is a research paradigm in which subjects are provided an opportunity to commit a "crime" (such as cheating) or asked to role-play a suspect. Subjects would be randomly assigned; those who are known to be guilty or innocent, or instructed as such, could then be questioned using the techniques of either minimization or maximization. We hypothesize that the results of well-designed studies would lead the criminal justice system to be concerned with these subtle ways of communicating messages of threats or promises.

A second manifestation of the functional equivalence of threats/promises and maximization/minimization is their possible impact on the jury. Previous research has shown that mock jurors react with ambivalence to confessions elicited by positive forms of inducement. Along the same lines, those prompted by minimization offer prosecuting attorneys a particularly potent weapon in the courtroom. If the subjects in the research reported in Chapter 6 are any standard, jurors who are confronted with this evidence will concede that the confession is "involuntary" by law, but they may also see the police interrogator as "sympathetic, not particularly eager for a confession, and suspicious if not actually informed about the defendant's culpability" (Kassin & McNall, 1991, p. 249). That is, minimization leads people to view the interrogation as noncoercive, a situation in which few truly innocent suspects are likely to confess.

Furthermore, minimization may even give rise to jurors' assuming that the interrogator must "have the goods" on the defendant. Like the trial lawyer who tarnishes a witness by asking questions that contain damaging presumptions (e.g., "when did you stop beating your wife?"), the interrogator who makes mitigating remarks may well communicate a presumption of guilt to jurors presented with that evidence (Kassin, Williams, & Saunders, 1990).

Additional research is needed to understand both the interrogation tactics that lead suspects to make self-incriminating statements and the effects these statements have on trial judges and juries. Which aspects of minimization and maximization ploys are most effective? Maximization, as defined in the experiments in Chapter 6, includes tactics designed to alter both the suspect's subjective likelihood of conviction and his or her sentencing expectations. Also, minimization includes tactics designed not only to alter sentencing expectations but to establish the police interrogator as the suspect's confidential ally, as in the Bradley Page case described in Chapter 7.

Further research is thus needed to isolate the effects of these different components, as well as to evaluate the possible coercive effects of other interrogation devices (e.g., the "good-cop, bad-cop" routine, the number of police interrogators present, the use of a combination of maximization and minimization).

References

Adams, R., Hoffer, W., & Hoffer, M. M. (1991). *Adams v. Texas.* New York: St. Martin's.

Annin, P. (1990, December 10). Unfriendly persuasion. *Newsweek,* p. 73.

Arizona v. Fulminante, 111 S. Ct. 1246 (1991).

Aronson, E. (1990, November). *Subtle coercion during police interrogation: The Bradley Page murder trial.* Invited address, Williams College, Williamstown, MA.

Asch, S. E. (1958). Effects of group pressure upon modification and distortion of judgments. In E. E. Maccoby, T. M. Newcomb, & E. L. Hartley (Eds.), *Readings in social psychology* (3rd ed.). New York: Holt, Rinehart & Winston.

Ashcraft v. Tennessee, 322 U.S. 143 (1944).

Associated Press. (1989, January 1). Did an innocent man serve another's time? *Kansas City Star,* p. 33A.

Aubry, A., & Caputo, R. (1965). *Criminal interrogation.* Springfield, IL: Charles C Thomas.

Baldwin, J., & McConville, M. (1980). *Confessions in Crown Court trials* [Study No. 5]. London: Royal Commission on Criminal Procedure.

Barthel, J. (1976). *A death in Canaan.* New York: E. P. Dutton.

Bedau, H., & Radelet, M. (1987). Miscarriages of justice in potentially capital cases. *Stanford Law Review, 40,* 21-179.

Bem, D. J. (1966). Inducing belief in false confessions. *Journal of Personality and Social Psychology, 3,* 707-710.

Bem, D. J. (1967, June). When saying is believing. *Psychology Today, 1*(2), 21-25.

Blackburn v. Alabama, 361 U.S. 199 (1960).

Borchard, E. M. (1932). *Convicting the innocent: Errors of criminal justice.* New Haven, CT: Yale University Press.

Bramel, D. (1969). Determinants of beliefs about other people. In J. Mills (Ed.), *Experimental social psychology.* New York: Macmillan.

Brandon, R., & Davies, C. (1972). *Wrongful imprisonment: Mistaken convictions and their consequences.* London: Allen & Unwin.

146

Brigham, J. C. (1992). A personal account of the research expert in court. *Contemporary Psychology, 37,* 529-530.

Broeder, D. (1959). The University of Chicago jury project. *Nebraska Law Review, 38,* 744-760.

Brown v. Mississippi, 297 U.S. 278 (1936).

Bruton v. United States, 391 U.S. 123 (1968).

Buckhout, R. (1986). Personal values and expert testimony. *Law and Human Behavior, 10,* 127-144.

Chambers v. Florida, 309 U.S. 727 (1940).

Chapman v. California, 386 U.S. 18 (1967).

Colorado v. Connelly, 479 U.S. 157 (1986).

Committee on Model Jury Instructions, Ninth Circuit. (1992). *Manual of model criminal jury instructions for the Ninth Circuit.* St. Paul, MN: West.

Coyle, M., & Lavell, M. (1991, April 8). Enigmatic Souter sides with conservatives. *National Law Journal,* pp. 5, 27.

Cruz v. New York, 481 U.S. 186 (1987).

Culombe v. Connecticut, 367 U.S. 568 (1961).

DeConingh v. State, 433 So. 2d 501 (Fla. 1983).

Deeley, P. (1971). *Beyond the breaking point.* London: Arthur Barker Ltd.

DePaulo, B. M., & Pfeifer, R. L. (1986). On-the-job experience and skill in detecting deception. *Journal of Applied Social Psychology, 16,* 249-267.

DePaulo, B. M., Stone, J. I., & Lassiter, G. D. (1985). Deceiving and detecting deceit. In B. R. Schlenker (Ed.), *The self and social life* (pp. 323-370). New York: McGraw-Hill.

DeVitt, E. J., Blackmar, C. B., Wolff, M. A., & O'Malley, K. F. (1987). *Federal jury practice and instructions.* St. Paul, MN: West.

Dicks, V. I. (1992, January). Voir dire: Pre-trial publicity. *Court Call,* pp. 1-3.

Dorsciak v. Gladden, 246 Ore. 233, 425 P.2d 177 (1967).

Driver, E. D. (1968). Confessions and the social psychology of coercion. *Harvard Law Review, 82,* 42-61.

Earl of Birkenhead, The. (Ed.). (1938). *More famous trials.* London: Hutchinson & Co.

Ekman, P., & O'Sullivan, M. (1991). Who can catch a liar? *American Psychologist, 46,* 913-920.

Elwork, A., Sales, B. D., & Alfini, J. J. (1977). Juridic decisions: In ignorance of the law or in light of it? *Law and Human Behavior, 1,* 163-189.

Escobedo v. Illinois, 378 U.S. 478 (1964).

Fleming, J. H., & Scott, B. A. (1991). The costs of confession: The Persian Gulf War POW tapes in historical and theoretical perspective. *Contemporary Social Psychology, 15*(4), 127-138.

Fletcher, G. P. (1988). *A crime of self-defense: Bernhard Goetz and the law on trial.* New York: Free Press.

Foster, H. H. (1969). Confessions and the station house syndrome. *Depaul Law Review, 18,* 683-701.

Frank, J. (1949). *Courts on trial.* Princeton, NJ: Princeton University Press.

Franklin, C. (1970). *The third degree.* London: Robert Hale.

Friedrich, O. (1987, June 29). "Not guilty." *Time,* pp. 10-11.

Frye v. United States, 293 F. 1013, 34 A.L.R. 154 (D.C.Cir.) (1923).

148 CONFESSIONS IN THE COURTROOM

Fulero, S. M. (1988, August). *Eyewitness expert testimony: An overview and annotated bibliography, 1931-1988.* Paper presented at the annual meeting of the American Psychological Association, Atlanta.

Gilbert, D. T., & Jones, E. E. (1986). Perceiver-induced constraint: Interpretations of self-generated reality. *Journal of Personality and Social Psychology, 50,* 269-280.

Goleman, D. (1992, July 21). Childhood trauma: Memory or invention? *The New York Times,* p. B5.

Graham, F. P. (1970). *The due process revolution: The Warren Court impact on criminal law.* Rochelle Park, NY: Hayden.

Greenhouse, L. (1992, October 14). High court to decide admissibility of scientific evidence in U.S. courts. *The New York Times,* p. A9.

Gudjonsson, G. H. (1984a). Interrogative suggestibility comparison between "false confessions" and "deniers" in criminal trials. *Medicine, Science, and the Law, 24,* 56-60.

Gudjonsson, G. H. (1984b). A new scale of interrogative suggestibility. *Personality and Individual Differences, 5,* 303-314.

Gudjonsson, G. H. (1986). Historical background to suggestibility: How interrogative suggestibility differs from other types of suggestibility. *Personality and Individual Differences, 8,* 347-355.

Gudjonsson, G. H. (1987). A parallel form of the Gudjonsson Suggestibility Scale. *British Journal of Clinical Psychology, 26,* 215-221.

Gudjonsson, G. H. (1988). Interrogative suggestibility and its relationship with assertiveness, social anxiety, fear of negative evaluation and methods of coping. *British Journal of Clinical Psychology, 27,* 159-166.

Gudjonsson, G. H. (1989). Compliance in an interrogative situation: A new scale. *Personality and Individual Differences, 10,* 535-540.

Gudjonsson, G. H. (1990). One hundred alleged false confession cases: Some normative data. *British Journal of Clinical Psychology, 29,* 249-250.

Gudjonsson, G. H. (1991). The application of interrogative suggestibility to police interviewing. In J. F. Schumaker (Ed.), *Human suggestibility: Advances in theory, research, and application* (pp. 279-288). New York: Routledge.

Gudjonsson, G. H., & Clark, N. K. (1986). Suggestibility in police interrogation: A social psychological model. *Social Behavior, 1,* 83-104.

Gudjonsson, G. H., & Hilton, M. (1989). The effects of instructional manipulation on interrogative suggestibility. *Social Behavior, 4,* 189-193.

Gudjonsson, G. H., & MacKeith, J. A. C. (1988). Retracted confessions: Legal, psychological, and psychiatric aspects. *Medicine, Science, and the Law, 28,* 187-194.

Gudjonsson, G. H., & MacKeith, J. A. C. (1990). A proven case of false confession: Psychological aspects of the coerced-compliant type. *Medicine, Science, and the Law, 30,* 329-335.

Guttmacher, M., & Weihofen, H. (1952). *Psychiatry and the law.* New York: Norton.

Hale, M., Jr. (1980). *Human science and social order: Hugo Münsterberg and the origins of applied psychology.* Philadelphia: Temple University Press.

Hansdottir, I., Thorsteinsson, H. S., Kristinsdottir, H., & Ragnarsson, R. S. (1990). The effects of instructions and anxiety on interrogative suggestibility. *Personality and Individual Differences, 11,* 85-87.

Hilgard, E. R. (1975). Hypnosis. *Annual Review of Psychology, 26,* 19-44.

Holbrook, S. H. (1957). *Dreamers of the American dream.* Garden City, NY: Doubleday.

In re Walker, 10 Cal. 3d 764, 518 P. 2d 1129 (1974).

Inbau, F. E., & Reid, J. E. (1962). *Criminal interrogation and confessions.* Baltimore, MD: Williams & Wilkins.

Inbau, F. E., Reid, J. E., & Buckley, J. P. (1986). *Criminal interrogation and confessions* (3rd ed.). Baltimore, MD: Williams & Wilkins.

Irvin v. Dowd, 81 S. Ct. 1639 (1961).

Irving, B. L. (1980). *A case study of current practice* [Research Study No. 2]. London: Royal Commission on Criminal Procedure.

Irving, B. L., & Hilgendorf, E. L. (1980). *Police interrogation: The psychological approach* [Research Study No. 2]. London: Royal Commission on Criminal Procedure.

Jackson v. Denno, 378 U.S. 368 (1964).

Jones, E. E. (1990). *Interpersonal perception.* San Francisco: Freeman.

Jones, E. E., & Harris, V. A. (1967). The attribution of attitudes. *Journal of Experimental Social Psychology, 3,* 1-24.

Kagehiro, D. K., & Laufer, W. S. (Eds.). (1992). *Handbook of psychology and the law.* New York: Springer.

Kalven, H., & Zeisel, H. (1966). *The American jury.* Boston: Little, Brown.

Kaplan, M. F., & Miller, L. E. (1978). Reducing the effects of juror bias. *Journal of Personality and Social Psychology, 36,* 1443-1455.

Kassin, S. M., Ellsworth, P. C., & Smith, V. L. (1989). The "general acceptance" of psychological research on eyewitness testimony: A survey of the experts. *American Psychologist, 44,* 1089-1098.

Kassin, S. M., & McNall, K. (1991). Police interrogations and confessions: Communicating promises and threats by pragmatic implication. *Law and Human Behavior, 15,* 233-251.

Kassin, S. M., Williams, L. N., & Saunders, C. L. (1990). Dirty tricks of cross examination: The influence of conjectural evidence on the jury. *Law and Human Behavior, 14,* 373-384.

Kassin, S. M., & Wrightsman, L. S. (1979). On the requirements of proof: The timing of judicial instruction and mock juror verdicts. *Journal of Personality and Social Psychology, 37,* 1877-1887.

Kassin, S. M., & Wrightsman, L. S. (1980). Prior confessions and mock juror verdicts. *Journal of Applied Social Psychology, 10,* 133-146.

Kassin, S. M., & Wrightsman, L. S. (1981). Coerced confessions, judicial instruction, and mock juror verdicts. *Journal of Applied Social Psychology, 11,* 489-506.

Kassin, S. M., & Wrightsman, L. S. (1985). Confession evidence. In S. Kassin & L. Wrightsman (Eds.), *The psychology of evidence and trial procedure* (pp. 67-94). Beverly Hills, CA: Sage.

Kaufman, E. (1966, October 2). The confession debate continues. *The New York Times Magazine,* p. 50.

Kelley, H. H. (1971). *Attribution in social interaction.* Morristown, NJ: General Learning Press.

Kelman, H. C. (1958). Compliance, identification, and internalization: Three processes of opinion change. *Journal of Conflict Resolution, 2,* 51-60.

Kerr, N. L., Atkin, R. S., Stasser, G., Meek, D., Holt, R. W., & Davis, J. H. (1976). Guilt beyond a reasonable doubt: Effects of concept definition and assigned decision rule on the judgments of mock jurors. *Journal of Personality and Social Psychology, 34,* 282-294.

Kinkead, E. (1959). *In every war but one.* New York: Norton.

Kramer, G. P., Kerr, N. L., & Carroll, J. S. (1990). Pretrial publicity, judicial remedies, and jury bias. *Law and Human Behavior, 14,* 409-438.

Kruglanski, A. W., & Cohen, M. (1974). Attributing freedom in the decision context: Effects of the choice alternatives, degree of commitment and predecision uncertainty. *Journal of Personality and Social Psychology, 30,* 178-187.

Lacayo, R. (1991, April 8). Confessions that were taboo are now just a technicality. *Time,* pp. 26-27.

Lassiter, G. D., & Irvine, A. A. (1986). Videotaped confession: The impact of camera point of view on judgments of coercion. *Journal of Applied Social Psychology, 16,* 268-276.

Lego v. Twomey, 404 U.S. 477 (1972).

Leo, R. A. (1992). From coercion to deception: The changing nature of police interrogation in America. *Crime, Law, and Social Change, 18,* 35-39.

Lepper, M. R. (1983). Social control processes, and the internalization of social values: An attributional perspective. In E. T. Higgins, D. N. Ruble, & W. W. Hartup (Eds.), *Social cognition and social development: A sociocultural perspective* (pp. 294-330). Cambridge: Cambridge University Press.

Lewis, A. (1991, April 26). Court in a hurry. *The New York Times,* p. A15.

Lisenba v. California, 314 U.S. 219 (1941).

Lloyd-Bostock, S. (1989). *Law in practice.* Chicago: Lyceum.

Loftus, E. F. (1983). Silence is not golden. *American Psychologist, 65,* 9-15.

Loftus, E. F. (1992, August). *The reality of repressed memories.* Invited address presented at the annual meetings of the American Psychological Association, Washington, D.C.

Loftus, E. F., & Ketcham, K. (1991). *Witness for the defense.* New York: St. Martin's.

Los Angeles Times. (1992, July 27). Killings by police alleged. *Kansas City Star,* p. A-3.

Lyons v. Oklahoma, 322 U.S. 596 (1944).

Macdonald, J. M., & Michaud, D. L. (1987). *The confession: Interrogation and criminal profiles for police officers.* Denver: Apache.

Malloy v. Hogan, 378 U.S. 1 (1964).

Marx, G. T. (1988). *Undercover: Police surveillance in America.* Berkeley: University of California Press.

Massiah v. United States, 377 U.S. 201 (1964).

Mathes, W. C., & DeVitt, E. J. (1965). *Federal jury practice and instructions.* St. Paul, MN: West.

McCormick, C. T. (1946). Some problems and developments in the admissibility of confessions. *Texas Law Review, 24,* 239-245.

McCormick, C. T. (1972). *Handbook of the law of evidence* (2nd ed.). St. Paul, MN: West.

Milgram, S. (1974). *Obedience to authority.* New York: Harper & Row.

Miller, A. G., Jones, E. E., & Hinkle, S. (1981). A robust attribution error in the personality domain. *Journal of Experimental Social Psychology, 17,* 587-600.

Miller, G. R., & Boster, F. J. (1977). Three images of the trial: Their implications for psychological research. In B. Sales (Ed.), *Psychology in the legal process.* New York: Halsted.

Miranda v. Arizona, 384 U.S. 436 (1966).

Mitchell, B. (1983, September). Confessions and police interrogation of suspects. *Criminal Law Review,* pp. 596-604.

Moran v. Burbine, 475 U.S. 412 (1986).

Moston, S., & Moston, T. (1991, April). *Challenging the obvious?: Suspect behavior during police questioning.* Paper presented at the meetings of the British Psychological Society, Bournemouth, UK.

Moston, S., Stephenson, G. M., & Williamson, T. M. (1991). The effects of case characteristics on suspect behavior during police questioning. *British Journal of Criminology.*

Mullin, C. (1986). *Error of judgement: The Birmingham bombings.* London: Chatto & Windus.

Mu'Min v. Virginia, 111 S. Ct. 1899 (1991).

Münsterberg, H. (1908). *On the witness stand.* Garden City, NY: Doubleday.

New York v. Quarles, 467 U.S. 649 (1984).

Nietzel, M. T., & Dillehay, R. C. (1986). *Psychological consultation in the courtroom.* Elmsford, NY: Pergamon.

Note. (1953). Voluntary false confessions: A neglected area in criminal administration. *Indiana Law Journal, 28,* 374-392.

Ofshe, R. (1992). Inadvertent hypnosis during interrogation: False confession due to dissociative state, misidentified multiple personality, and the satanic cult hypothesis. *International Journal of Clinical and Experimental Hypnosis, 40,* 125-156.

O'Hara, C. E., & O'Hara, G. L. (1956). *Fundamentals of criminal investigation.* Springfield, IL: Charles C Thomas.

O'Hara, C. E., & O'Hara, G. L. (1980). *Fundamentals of criminal investigation* (5th ed.). Springfield, IL: Charles C Thomas.

Patton v. Yount, 467 U.S. 1025 (1984).

Paulsen, M. G. (1954). The Fourteenth Amendment and the third degree. *Stanford Law Review, 6,* 411-437.

Payne v. Arkansas, 356 U.S. 560 (1958).

Pennebaker, J. W. (1987, Spring). Healthy talk. *SMU Mustang,* pp. 13-15.

Pennebaker, J. W. (1990). *Opening up: The healing power of confiding in others.* New York: Morrow.

People v. Hartgraves, 1 Cal. App. 3d, 117 (1964).

People v. Thompson, 266 Cal. Rptr. 309, 785 p. 2d 857 (1990).

People v. Trout, 54 Cal. 2d 576, 354 p. 2d 231 (1960).

People v. Watkins, 6 Cal. App. 3d 119 (1970).

Pratkanis, A. R., & Aronson, E. (1991). *Age of propaganda: The everyday use and abuse of persuasion.* New York: Freeman.

Press, A. (1987, June 29). A trial that wouldn't end. *Newsweek,* pp. 20-21.

Reik, T. (1959). *The compulsion to confess.* New York: Farrar, Straus, & Giroux.

Rogers v. Richmond, 365 U.S. 534 (1961).

Rogge, O. J. (1959). *Why men confess.* New York: Da Capo Press.

Ross, L. (1977). The intuitive psychologist and his shortcomings: Distortions in the attribution process. In L. Berkowitz (Ed.), *Advances in experimental social psychology* (Vol. 10). San Diego: Academic Press.

Royal, R. F., & Schutt, S. R. (1976). *The gentle art of interviewing and interrogation: A professional manual and guide.* Englewood Cliffs, NJ: Prentice-Hall.

Savage, M. (1970). *A great fall.* New York: Simon & Schuster.

152   CONFESSIONS IN THE COURTROOM

Schein, E. H. (1956). The Chinese indoctrination program for prisoners of war: A study of attempted "brainwashing." *Psychiatry, 19,* 149-172.

Schein, E. H., Schneier, I., & Barker, C. H. (1961). *Coercive persuasion: A sociopsychological analysis of the "brainwashing" of American civilian prisoners by Chinese Communists.* New York: Norton.

Sherif, M. (1935). A study of some social factors in perception. *Archives of Psychology, 27,* No. 187, 1-60.

Simon, R. J., & Mahan, J. (1971). Quantifying burdens of proof: A view from the bench, the jury, and the classroom. *Law and Society Review, 6,* 319-330.

Slough, M. C. (1959). Confessions and admissions. *Fordham Law Review, 28,* 96-114.

Spivak, J. (1988, December 18). Retarded man still denies guilt in 2-year-old murder conviction. *Kansas City Star,* p. 31A.

State v. Cervantes, 814 P. 2d 1232 (1991).

State v. Jackson, 304 S. E. 2d 134 (1983).

State v. Kelly, 376 A. 2d 840 (Me, 1977).

Stein v. New York, 346 U.S. 156 (1953).

Stephens, O. H., Jr. (1973). *The Supreme Court and confessions of guilt.* Knoxville: University of Tennessee Press.

Sue, S., Smith, R. E., & Caldwell, C. (1973). Effects of inadmissible evidence on the decisions of simulated jurors: A moral dilemma. *Journal of Applied Social Psychology, 3,* 345-353.

The Supreme Court's harmful error. *The New York Times.* (1991, March 29). [Editorial], p. A12.

Sutherland, A. E. (1965). Crime and confession. *Harvard Law Review, 79,* 21-41.

Taylor, S., Jr. (1988, June 16). Court reaffirms limits in questioning of suspects. *New York Times,* p. 9.

Taylor, S. E., & Fiske, S. T. (1978). Salience, attention, and attribution: Top of the head phenomena. In L. Berkowitz (Ed.), *Advances in experimental social psychology* (Vol. 2, pp. 249-288). San Diego: Academic Press.

Thibaut, J., & Walker, L. (1975). *Procedural justice: A psychological analysis.* New York: Erlbaum/Halstead.

Townsend v. Sain, 372 U.S. 293 (1963).

United States v. Bradshaw, 840 Fzd 871 (1988).

United States v. Mitchell, 322 U.S. 65 (1944).

U.S. National Commission on Law Observance and Enforcement. (1931). *Report on lawlessness in law enforcement.* Washington, DC: Government Printing Office.

Vidal-Naquet, P. (1963). *Torture: Cancer of democracy, France and Algeria, 1954-62.* Baltimore, MD: Penguin.

W. M. v. State (Florida). WL 152501 (Fla. App. 4 Dist.) (1991).

Wald, M., Ayres, R., Hess, D. W., Schantz, M., & Whitebread, C. H. (1967). Interrogations in New Haven: The impact of Miranda. *Yale Law Journal, 76,* 1519-1648.

Weiner, B., Graham, S., Peter, O., & Zmuidinas, M. (1991). Public confession and forgiveness. *Journal of Personality, 59,* 281-312.

Weinstein, E., Abrams, S., & Gibbons, D. (1970). The validity of the polygraph with hypnotically induced repression and guilt. *American Journal of Psychiatry, 126,* 1159-1162.

Wells, G. L. (1980). Asymmetric attributions for compliance: Reward vs. punishment. *Journal of Experimental Social Psychology, 16,* 47-60.

Wells, G. L. (1984). How adequate is human intuition for judging eyewitness testimony? In G. L. Wells & E. F. Loftus (Eds.), *Eyewitness testimony: Psychological perspectives* (pp. 256-272). Cambridge, MA: Cambridge University Press.

Wells, G. L. (1986). Expert psychological testimony: Empirical and conceptual analysis of effects. *Law and Human Behavior, 10,* 83-95.

White, W. S. (1979). Police trickery in inducing confessions. *University of Pennsylvania Law Review, 127,* 581-629.

Wigmore, J. H. (1937). *The science of judicial proof.* Boston: Little, Brown.

Wigmore, J. H. (1970). *Evidence in trials at common law* (Vol. 3). (Rev. by J. H. Chadbourn). Boston: Little, Brown.

Wolf, S., & Montgomery, D. A. (1977). Effects of inadmissible evidence and level of judicial admonishment to disregard on the judgments of mock jurors. *Journal of Applied Social Psychology, 7,* 205-219.

Younger, E. J. (1966). Interrogation of criminal defendants—Some views on Miranda v. Arizona. *Fordham Law Review, 35,* 255-262.

Zimbardo, P. G. (1967, June). The psychology of police confessions. *Psychology Today, 1*(2), 17-20, 25-27.

Name Index

Subject Index

About the Authors

Lawrence S. Wrightsman (Ph.D., University of Minnesota, 1959) is Professor of Psychology at the University of Kansas, Lawrence. He is an author or editor of 17 books, about half of which deal with criminal justice issues. These include *Psychology and the Legal System* (1991), *The American Jury on Trial* (1988), *In the Jury Box* (1987), *On the Witness Stand* (1987), *The Psychology of Evidence and Trial Procedure* (1985), *The Child Witness* (1991), and *Rape: The Misunderstood Crime* (1993). He has been doing research on legal processes for almost 20 years and is director of the Kansas Jury Project. He has testified as an expert witness on the issue of accuracy of eyewitness identification, and he has assisted defense attorneys in jury selection in various types of trials ranging from criminal murder cases to civil malpractice suits. At the 1989 convention of the American Psychological Association he gave the first G. Stanley Hall Lecture devoted to the topic of psychology and the law. He is a former President of the Society for the Psychological Study of Social Issues and of the Society of Personality and Social Psychology.

Saul M. Kassin (Ph.D., University of Connecticut, 1978) is Professor of Psychology at Williams College, Williamstown, MA. He was an NIMH Postdoctoral Research Fellow in the Psychology and Law Program at Stanford University (1985-1986) and was awarded a U.S.

163

Supreme Court Judicial Fellowship (1984-1985), serving as a research associate at the Federal Judicial Center in Washington, DC. He is the author or editor of six other books, including *The Psychology of Evidence and Trial Procedure* (1985), *On the Witness Stand* (1987), *In the Jury Box* (1987), and *The American Jury on Trial* (1988). His numerous articles and book chapters deal with the topics of evidence, trial procedure, and jury decision making. He has worked with lawyers as a trial consultant and has testified as an expert on eyewitness testimony and coerced confessions.

Sara L. Bloom (J.D., University of Kansas, 1992) is an associate with a law firm in the Baltimore, MD, area, with emphasis on litigation. She received her bachelor of arts degree as well as her law degree at the University of Kansas. Previously she was employed in the prosecutor's office in Miami/Dade County, FL.